THE STORY OF COUNTRY MUSIC

COLIN ESCOTT

BBC

This book is published to accompany the television series *Lost Highway*,
which was first broadcast on BBC Television in 2003.
Executive producer: Michael Poole
Producer: William Naylor
Directors: Ben Southwell, Sally Thomson, Andrew Graham-Brown, and Ian Pye
Production manager: Kate Slattery
Production assistant: George Harwood
Researchers: Simon Ashley and Lisa Drake
Assistant producer: Sebastian Barfield
Archive researcher: Declan Smith

ISBN 0 563 48820 4

Published by BBC Worldwide Ltd,
Woodlands, 80 Wood Lane, London W12 0TT

Commissioning editor: Emma Shackleton
Project editor: Patricia Burgess
Art director: Linda Blakemore
Designer: Annette Peppis
Picture research: Colin Escott and David Cottingham
Production controller: Kenneth McKay

Set in Rosewood and Frutiger
Printed and bound in Great Britain by Butler & Tanner Ltd, Frome
Colour separations by Radstock Reproductions Ltd, Midsomer Norton
Jacket printed by Lawrence-Allen Ltd, Weston-super-Mare

previous page Saturday night at *The Grand Ole Opry*.

contents

foreword

I'm a rolling stone, all alone and lost
For a life of sin, I have paid the cost,
When I pass by, all the people say
"Just another guy on the lost highway."

A verse sometimes says so much. Many of country music's recurring themes are there: isolation, perdition, and rootlessness. And it's those recurring themes that we've tried to uncover in this book and in the BBC television series of the same name.

Anyone who remembers Monty Python's "Summarize Proust" sketch will have some idea of the difficulty in capturing the story of country music in a few words and images, but in all the discussions preceding the series and the book we wanted to do more than simply recount the big artists and big hits. We wanted to underscore the turning points: the moments when the music changed a little, for better or worse.

The book doesn't entirely mirror the television series, although it draws on the interviews conducted for it. Many of the shared viewpoints came out in lengthy discussions with the series producer, William Naylor, and the *Lost Highway* production team. The fact that the series was produced by the BBC in England also gave us an excuse to unravel the connection between traditional British music and American country music, and the very different ways in which Europeans and Americans now understand country music. The links between the old and new worlds are tenuous, but intriguing. For instance, the BBC series was produced in Bristol, England, while the first epochal country sessions were held in Bristol, Tennessee (and Bristol, England, was the birthplace of one of country music's first great producers, Arthur Satherley).

And on a stiflingly humid night in Tennessee, it's still possible to attend a back-porch bluegrass jam and hear a jig or hornpipe that crossed from a chilly island several hundred years earlier.

I'd like to thank William Naylor for recommending me to Emma Shackleton, commissioning editor at BBC Worldwide. I began this book thirty-two years after getting off the Greyhound bus in Nashville, hopeful of understanding the music that had so intrigued me from afar. I've learned much in the interceding years. Sometimes I've despaired about country music's future, and sometimes I've been heartened, but above all this book and the discussions with William Naylor and his staff have been a wonderful opportunity to decide what's truly important.

Many of the photos that accompany the text are previously unpublished, and I'd especially like to thank Brenda Colladay at *The Grand Ole Opry* archives, Richard Weize at Bear Family Records, and David Booth at Showtime Music Archives for sharing the images that help tell the story. Thanks also to Eddie Stubbs and Kevin Coffey for looking over portions of the text.

Over the years, hundreds of people have told me their stories. In most cases, I offered nothing but genuine and unaffected interest. Every piece of music is someone's story. We begin with educated guesses about lives revealed to us in tantalizing fragments, and close in the age of plenty. It's too easy to say that earlier generations should have taken more notice of this music. I'm as guilty. I've met people, then failed to ask questions I later dearly wish I'd asked. The opportunity, of course, has now passed.

The houses I knew as a child always seemed to have dark corridors. And it's in dark places that we begin – trying to shine a little light on early America.

Colin Escott
Nashville, Tennessee
September 2002

introduction

Such music could only be produced by a life of
unimaginable harshness. When Dock Boggs and his
buddy Hub Mahaffey went to record for Brunswick
Records in 1927, they opened a window onto a closed-
off world. In a few foxed and faded photographs, and
in verses like the ones below, we see deeply, maybe
too deeply, into turn-of-the-century Appalachia.

"Oh Willie, oh Willie, I'm afraid of your way
Your mind is to ramble and lead me astray."

"Pretty Polly, Pretty Polly, you're guessing 'bout right.
I dug on your grave two thirds of last night."

Dock Boggs' part of Virginia had been settled for 150 years by the time he was
born in 1898. The settlements around his birthplace bore names such as
Needmore, which really told their own story. The names in the cemetery were
almost exclusively English, Irish, and Scots, but those interred were not the
sons and daughters of Albion. Not anymore. Something happened in the
darkness and isolation of Appalachia—something that transformed the songs
brought over from the old country, just as it transformed the migrants. "Pretty
Polly" was an old British ballad originally called "The Cruel Ship's Carpenter,"
but nothing captured in England in the early part of the century was as bleak
and unforgiving as Dock Boggs' performance of "Pretty Polly." Critic Greil
Marcus remarked that he sang as if "his bones were coming through his skin

every time he opened his mouth." The music of the old country survived almost intact in parts of Canada, especially Nova Scotia and Newfoundland, but in Appalachia it was warped and hardened by the American experience.

Country music is quintessentially American. It borrowed from everywhere, yet became much greater than the sum of its parts. Art and commerce have done battle throughout its history, and commerce has usually won. Country music seems to live in fear of fulfilling Alfred Tennyson's prophecy, "Plenty corrupts the melody that made thee famous once," yet it has chased "plenty" for most of its lifespan. One hundred years after Dock Boggs' birth, country music was reckoned to be the most popular music in the United States. Scans at millions of computerized checkouts confirmed it. Country music had finally won its mass audience, but what had it lost? Its strangeness and its soul, perhaps. Dock Boggs' songs of death and dismemberment seemed not at all strange to him; they were just part of life as it was lived. Dolly Parton's hair, teased a foot above her head, didn't seem strange to her; the higher the hair, the closer to God. But the strangeness slowly ebbed from country music, just as it slowly ebbed from Southern society. The strangeness disappeared along with the South's apartness. In Southern towns too small to support the chain stores, it's still possible to see or infer some of what Dock Boggs or Hank Williams saw, but too often a Southern town could be any town.

But then, at the 2002 Grammy Awards, bluegrass patriarch Ralph Stanley sang "O Death," a song that Dock Boggs might well have sung. The fact that Stanley was there at all says much for the enduring power of the old music, and probably says even more about the emotional poverty of the other nominees in the "Best Country" category. The fact

that Ralph Stanley is back on Columbia Records fifty years after he was dropped by the same label for being out of date is another testament to the power of unvarnished country music to touch people. The Grammy awards that Ralph Stanley brought back to Virginia won't change the way music is made in Nashville. They only confirm that country music is in one of its many soul-searching moments. Where now? The answer has always appeared, whether in the form of a family trio posting little signs outside their schoolhouse concerts stating "The program is morally good," or in the form of a chubby Oklahoman who moved his show from city to city in twenty trailers and buses, bringing all the trappings of stadium rock to country music.

opposite Dock Boggs.

SEIZE THE
Palpitating Air

If record companies had gone to New Orleans in the late nineteenth century, perhaps we could understand how freed slaves and Creoles picked up instruments left by Confederate marching bands and began improvising, thus creating jazz. Instead, there's a gaping hole. We don't quite know what happened.

If recording companies or enterprising folklorists had gone into small towns, hill communities, and hollers throughout the southeast during the eighteenth and nineteenth centuries, we might understand how the music of the old and new worlds melted into one. We might understand how parlor songs and minstrel music made their way into isolated rural communities. We might see how black performers introduced the banjo and the blues to white performers. We might understand how the cadences and melodies and fervor of religious music slipped into secular music. We might, in other words, know how country music came into being.

All but a few saw the music of the rural South as unworthy of study. British folklorist Cecil Sharp visited the United States several times between 1916 and 1918, traveling the South to compile his monumental work *English Folk Songs from the Southern Appalachians*. Sharp, though, arrived with an agenda. He wanted to prove that the songs of the old country survived more or less intact in the New World. In fact, they hadn't, and Sharp makes intriguing little asides that say more than he intended. "When by chance the text of a modern street song succeeds in penetrating into the mountains, it is at once mated to a

above Ira Louvin.
opposite Back-porch musicians in Appalachia during the 1930s.

traditional tune and sometimes still further purified by being molded into the form of a traditional ballad." This was just as true forty or fifty years later when folklorists finally tried to capture what was left of traditional mountain music, only to discover that they were often hearing a current Nashville hit reconfigured to sound as if it had crossed from England in the seventeenth century. It had happened all along.

Some songs certainly survived from the old country, and were handed down, but we'll never truly understand what happened to them. For example, the bluegrass classic "Little Joe" has a line, "What will Thomas the old gardener say," that doesn't seem to have much to do with the Appalachian experience. It's like looking at crumbling stone walls in Tennessee and imagining the early settlers from northern England or Scotland building them as their ancestors had taught them. Tantalizing vestiges remain. To complicate the picture, some songs came over during the late nineteenth century, not with immigrants but with British music-hall entertainers, who were very popular in some areas of the country before the First World War.

The instruments came from the Old World, both Europe and Africa. The fiddle came from Europe, as did the dulcimer and the mandolin, but the banjo came from black musicians in the nineteenth century. In 1781, Thomas Jefferson remarked, "The instrument proper to the slaves is the banjar which they brought hither from Africa." What Jefferson saw was a gourd covered in animal hide with a simple neck and several gut strings. By the late nineteenth century, the banjo was mass-produced and fairly common throughout

above The Blue Sky Boys.
opposite The Louvin Brothers.

the South. Mail-order catalogs began reaching into the South around 1900, hastening the spread of cheap, easy-to-learn, and easy-to-ship instruments. The hard, clipped notes of the banjo seemed to fit mountain music, as did the fiddle. Played slightly out of tune (as it nearly always was), the fiddle seemed an almost human cry. Fiddle, banjo, and the occasional mandolin or guitar were what you would have heard around 1900. The steel guitar didn't come into country music until later. Its predecessor, the unamplified Hawaiian-style slide guitar, made its way into country music in the late 1920s, and the electric steel guitar followed in the mid-1930s.

In 1959, folklorist Alan Lomax went in search of early music in the southern uplands, and brought a keen insight to his discoveries. He'd spent most of the 1950s in England, and knew enough about British traditional music to appreciate what had happened to it in its new home. "The ancient ballads linked the pioneers with their British homeland," he wrote, "and kept alive ancient patterns of emotion and poetry that beautified their lives. The singers, however, did not regard them as historical documents, but as dramas, which exemplified traits of character…that they perceived in themselves and their neighbors. [The] singers

rarely make a distinction between old and new ballads." Sometimes, listening to the folkloric recordings made by Lomax and others, you can close your eyes and believe that you're hearing music as it was played up in the hills and down in the hollers long before the "talking machine" came along. Lomax was quick to point out the American contribution to the music. For one thing, it was sung unlike British folk music. The strangled, nasal vocals were as uniquely American as the banjo. Never short of a theory, Lomax figured that the "narrow voiced" singing came from "the emotional tensions of frontier Protestantism with its painful sanctions against fleshly pleasure."

String bands were the prevailing sound in early music, but were soon eclipsed by brother duets. At its lamest, the duet is simply two people singing together, but at its best there's an empathy that almost defies analysis. One partner will intuitively know where the other is going. If one goes high, the other will go low, and in between there's a ghostly overtone that's almost a third voice. Years of back-porch practice meant that the best duet acts were almost always brothers, and they almost always played string instruments that meshed as flawlessly as the vocals. The Delmore Brothers were very popular from the time they joined *The Grand*

Ole Opry in 1933 until the late 1940s, but the Blue Sky Boys (Bill and Earl Bolick) remain the quintessential brother act. Their stage name was strangely at odds with their music: even their most joyous songs seemed to have a dark undercurrent. The Bolicks were from rural North Carolina. Bill played mandolin and sang tenor; Earl played guitar and sang baritone. In 1936, they recorded the old murder ballad "On the Banks of the Ohio," bringing all its eeriness to the surface. When they sing "Come my love, let's take a walk, just a little ways away," it carries a dreadful premonition of what is about to happen. The Bolicks fought, as all brother duets seemed destined to do, but regrouped occasionally into the 1960s.

The father of bluegrass, Bill Monroe, began his career in a singing brother act, and formulated many of his concepts during that time. The Louvin Brothers took the sound into the 1950s, and exercised a huge influence over cosmic cowboys such as Gram Parsons, and, through him, Emmylou Harris and alternative country. The Everly Brothers brought the country brother sound into the rock 'n' roll era. Instead of songs about death and perdition, there were more pressing concerns: "When Will I Be Loved?", "Should We Tell Him?", and "How Can I Meet Her?"

Out west, fiddle tunes prevailed. The fiddle belonged at every social gathering and every political meeting. Fiddle tunes became the foundation of western swing music, just as Appalachian music became the backbone of hillbilly and bluegrass music. One of the first country musicians to get onto record was Eck Robertson, who'd grown up in the Texas panhandle. In 1922, Robertson and his buddy, Civil War veteran Henry Gilliland, attended a

Confederate veterans reunion in Richmond, Virginia. Robertson had just seen a newsreel about the record business, and Gilliland happened to mention that he had a friend in New York who worked for RCA Victor (or the Victor Talking Machine Company, as it was called at the time), so they decided to board a train for New York. The Victor executives were sufficiently intrigued to record a dozen sides of Robertson's fiddle music. It's hard to know how well they sold. Robertson didn't record again until 1929, suggesting that he sold poorly, but other record companies immediately began recording fiddle players, suggesting quite the opposite. It had taken the record business forty-five years to discover country music.

Thomas Edison had invented the phonograph in 1877. The following year, he recorded a little salutation that he played at demonstrations:

I seize the palpitating air, I hoard
Music and speech. All lips that breathe are mine.

From the moment Victor seized Eck Robertson's palpitating air, country music and records would be forever entwined. Records captured all American ethnic music, not just country music. They captured the music, then hastened its demise.

Chapter 2

THE BRISTOL
Sessions

Before the First World War, the talking machine was a new toy for rich urbanites. Victor's top-of-the-line Victrola phonograph retailed at $200 (roughly $3800 today), and the catalogs were heavy on opera and parlor songs. Then, just as mass production was bringing the phonograph within reach of all, radio seemed to threaten the young industry.

But radio needed electricity, so phonograph manufacturers began mass-producing cheaper wind-up models for poorer homes without electricity. The phonograph manufacturers owned the record labels and sent their talent scouts in search of songs that would appeal to African-Americans, poor Southerners, and recent migrants.

In June 1923, New York-based OKeh Records sent A&R man Ralph Peer to Atlanta, Georgia. Pressured by the local OKeh dealer, Peer reluctantly agreed to record fifty-five-year-old Fiddlin' John Carson. In a 1938 interview with *Colliers* magazine Peer recalled what happened next. "We didn't even put a serial number on the record," he said, referring to Carson's "Little Old Log Cabin in the Lane." "[We thought] that when the local dealer got his supply that would be the end of it. We sent him 1000 records... That night he called New York and ordered 5000 more by express and 10,000 by freight. When the sales got up to 500,000 we were so ashamed we had Fiddlin' John come up to New York and do a re-recording." The figures might be overstated, but the pent-up demand was real enough. "The hill-billy thinks nothing of buying six or more of

above Ralph Peer.
opposite 408 State Street: site of the Bristol sessions.

the same record at 75c because of wear," reported Variety magazine in 1926. "The talking machine to the hill-billy is more practical than his Bible."

Ralph Peer switched allegiance to Victor in 1926, and the following summer he organized a trip to Bristol, Tennessee. It was early August 1927 when A. P. Carter read a little announcement in the *Bristol Herald-Courier*: "The Victor Co. will have a recording machine in Bristol for 10 days beginning Monday to record records." Peer himself was interviewed after he arrived. "In no section of the South have the pre-war melodies and old mountaineer songs been better preserved than in the mountains of east Tennessee," he told the paper. But the clincher came when he mentioned that another act he'd recorded nearby had received $3600 in royalties the previous year. People came off the mountains in droves. A. P. Carter led a family trio with his wife Sara, who was still nursing their youngest child, and Sara's young cousin Maybelle Addington. They borrowed a car and set off down the dirt roads of Clinch Mountain. A. P. planned to arrive by dusk, stay with his sister and rehearse, but once they reached the paved roads, the tires blew out and the road was so hot that the patches came off faster than A. P. could reattach them, so they arrived too late to do anything but go to bed. The following morning they went to the second floor of a hat factory where Peer had installed recording equipment. Quilts were hung around the walls to deaden the echo. Unlike the other artists waiting to audition, the Carters had no show clothes, but Peer knew he'd stumbled onto something as soon as he heard Sara's voice. "That was it," he said. "I knew it was going to be wonderful."

Taken together, the 300 songs that the original Carter Family recorded between 1927 and 1941 make a compelling statement. Urbanization was already a fact of life. Kids were leaving farms and they weren't coming back. The past wasn't a rural idyll, but that didn't stop people yearning for it. The Carter Family's collected works seem almost a lament for a paradise lost. A. P. rarely sang and didn't play an instrument; he just came in on a song ("bassin' in" he called it) when he felt like it, but he found the songs and took care of business. Maybelle sang a ghostly harmony to Sara's lead and played guitar. Generations of guitarists took their cue from her, even though she did no more than restate the melody on the bottom strings. Her solo on "Wildwood Flower" is probably the most replicated solo in country music. Sara sang matter-of-factly of caskets and early death. Her voice was artlessly affecting, and she sang with the confrontational truculence you would expect from someone who had grown up seeing all she'd seen. There are around 150 photographs of the original Carter Family, and Sara smiles in precisely one of them.

For many years, it was thought that the Carter Family's music was Anglo-Celtic ballads preserved in the isolation of Appalachia, but it was much more. It was Victorian parlor music, gospel songs, blues, topical ballads, and vaudeville numbers. Their theme song, "Keep on the Sunny Side," was a gospel song from 1899; "Wildwood Flower" was a vaudeville song from 1860; "Wabash Cannonball" was a pop tune published in 1905; "Worried Man Blues" was a prison song probably acquired from an itinerant blues singer; "Black Jack David" was an English ballad dating back centuries; and "Will the Circle Be Unbroken" was a gospel song published around 1907. The Carter Family made all this music one, and made it their own. More questionably, they copyrighted it as their own.

Compare "I'll Twine 'mid the Ringlets" as Maud Irving and J. P. Webster wrote it in 1860 with

opposite The Carter Family – Maybelle, Sara, and A. P.

LOOK!
Victor Artist
A. P. CARTER
and the
Carter Family
Will give a
MUSICAL PROGRAM
AT *Roseland Theater*
ON *Thursday August 1.*

The Program is Morally Good
Admission 15 and 25 Cents
A. P. CARTER, Mace Spring, Va.

"Wildwood Flower" as the Carter Family recorded and copyrighted it sixty-seven years later.

I'll twine 'mid the ringlets of my raven black hair
The lilies so pale and the roses so fair
The myrtle so bright with an emerald hue
And the pale aronatus with eyes of bright blue.

I'll think of him never, I'll be wildly gay
I'll charm every heart and the crowd I will sway
I'll live yet to see him regret the dark hour
When he won and neglected this frail wildwood flower.

I'll twine with my mingles and waving black hair
With the roses so red and the lilies so fair
And the myrtle so bright with emerald dew
The pale and the leader and eyes look like blue.

He taught me to love him and called me his flower
Blooming to cheer him through life's dreary hour
I'm longing to see him through life's darkest hour
He's gone and neglected his pale wildwood flower.

A. P. Carter mangled the words to the point that they mean hardly anything, yet *his* version is the one that has survived. There was something so plaintive and compelling in Sara's delivery and in Maybelle's elegant solo. In fact, it's Maybelle who provides the song's "hook" by repeating her solo between every verse.

The situation is cloudier still on the song that became the Carter Family's greatest hit, "Will the Circle Be Unbroken." Three artists recorded it *before* the Carter Family, yet A. P. Carter's adaptation is the one that everyone knows and it's his name in the composer credit today. Charles Gabriel took credit for the original version, but Gabriel invited people to send their poems to him, then bought them for a

pittance. Where does that leave A. P. Carter? Not really the author, yet more than an arranger. Carter also had to contend with Ralph Peer, who pressured his artists to produce original material. Peer received just one dollar a year in salary from Victor, and made his money from copyrighting his artists' songs. In their defense, Peer and Carter were operating in a world very unlike our own. They had no access to computerized song databases and the stakes were pitifully small. At the depth of the Depression some Carter Family records sold just 500 copies, netting A. P. Carter all of five or ten dollars in composer royalties. It's his unerring taste more than his conscious or unconscious plagiarism that really impresses itself. He traveled ceaselessly and heard thousands of songs, yet his ear for the forlorn led him to around 300, many of them still sung, and without him those songs would have disappeared. Jimmie Rodgers was not from anywhere near

opposite Jimmie Rodgers.

Bristol, Tennessee; he just happened to be there when he received word of Peer's auditions. Rodgers was the original kid with a guitar, and became country music's first star. Like the Carter Family, he amalgamated everything he'd heard, but the music he'd heard was very different from the music that the Carter Family had heard. Raised in Mississippi, Rodgers didn't draw on folk ballads so much as the work chants of black section crews, jazz, blues, Hawaiian music, and vaudeville. Music was often the last career option for the afflicted, and after Rodgers developed tuberculosis in 1924, he gave up his career as a brakeman to concentrate on music. His trademark blue yodel was often heard in place of an instrumental solo. Swiss yodels were cheery, but the blue yodel owed more to black field hollers and the lonesome tones of railroad whistles.

Rodgers recorded 110 songs between 1927 and his death just six years later. On one occasion, he was backed by Louis Armstrong, underscoring just how different he was from the Carter Family. Louis Armstrong with the Carter Family is unimaginable. At his last session, Rodgers sounds so breathless and enervated that it's painful to listen to the recordings. He knew he was dying and hoped those final songs would give his family some income after his death, but the Depression had taken a huge bite out of record sales. His earlier records had sold 400,000 or 500,000 copies, but the last record released during his lifetime, "Old Love Letters," sold just 1000 copies.

In place of the Carter Family's piety and grim resignation, Rodgers' music was populated by good-time pals one step ahead of the law, but still ready to shed a tear for mother and home. "Portland, Maine is just the same as sunny Tennessee/Any place I hang my hat is home, sweet home to me." He sang with an insouciant, almost insolent, drawl. The sentimental numbers were offset by rowdier

songs, such as "In the Jailhouse Now," "Waiting for a Train," "Travelin' Blues," and "T for Texas," that set the stage for honky-tonk music. Even the sadly prophetic "T.B. Blues" is delivered with no self-pity or regret. Rodgers' records not only influenced an entire generation of country singers, but sold well to African-Americans, many of whom had no idea that he was white. Kids wanted to be Jimmie Rodgers in a way that they did not want to be A. P. Carter. Gene Autry, Ernest Tubb, Lefty Frizzell, Hank Snow, and many others began as Jimmie Rodgers acolytes. The first (and so far only) release on Bob Dylan's Egyptian Records was a Rodgers tribute.

The music coalesced around the Carters and Jimmie Rodgers because they sold, and sales always commanded respect. The record business has always been blind to any color but green. Neither Jimmie Rodgers nor the Carter Family made country music's first million-selling disc, though. "The Prisoner's Song" was one of more than 1600 songs that Vernon Dalhart recorded between 1916 and 1939, but it's the only one for which he's remembered. It's a simple song that doesn't make much more sense than A. P. Carter's mangling of "I'll Twine 'mid the Ringlets." The verses lament the fact that the narrator is incarcerated, while the chorus begins "Please meet me tonight in the moonlight, please meet me tonight all alone." The final verse seems almost randomly tacked on: "I have a grand ship on the ocean, all mounted with silver and gold, and before my poor darling would suffer, that ship would be anchored and sold." Perhaps the song's enigma accounted in part for its appeal. Perhaps the lovely, lilting melody sold it. Dalhart's cousin Guy Massey claimed to have written it, but so did backing musician Carson Robison, and Massey's brother Robert. In fact, the verses were a jumble of old folk songs, while the chorus was from an 1826 British music-hall number, "Meet Me by Moonlight Alone."

Dalhart wasn't a country singer. He recorded everything from Gilbert & Sullivan to "coon" recitations, but "The Prisoner's Song" was his lucky break. He'd gone to Victor in 1924 to re-record his biggest hit to that point, "Wreck of the Old 97," when Guy Massey persuaded him to put "The Prisoner's Song" on the flip side. As confused as it was, it made Dalhart a star. The Strand Theater in New York paid him $3500 for a two-week stint, requiring him to sing just that one song, but he invested unwisely and died in 1948, working as a night clerk in a hotel in Bridgeport, Connecticut. Dalhart might not have been a country singer, but the million-plus copies (some say 6 million) that "The Prisoner's Song" sold opened the eyes of the record business to the potential of country music.

Records, meanwhile, opened the eyes of young performers to the world around them. It was no longer sufficient to be the best fiddler or singer for miles around; now there were records with tangible evidence of someone doing it better—often much better. Records were not only humbling, they were educative. Suddenly, it was possible for young guitarists like Arthur Smith, Zeb and Zeke Turner, and Hank Garland to grow up in rural South Carolina, yet study masters such as Django Reinhardt and Eddie Lang. Smith, Garland, and the Turners began making records in the 1930s and 1940s, sounding wholly unlike the first generation of country guitarists. Records cross-pollinated music with a speed that was unthinkable before their arrival.

For generations, country music had been non-commercial, passed down within families and communities. Records commodified it. Old songs became potential copyrights and the bands at the local barn dance became potential recording stars.

Records began drawing a line between performers and audiences. In earlier times, everyone might join in, but that was no longer the case. The experience of music had once been social, now it was solitary. Somewhere along the way, the professional country musician was born. Jimmie Rodgers and the Carter Family were among the first. Country music, once a weekend pursuit at best, was now a career option.

above Vernon Dalhart (right) with his accompanist and in-house songwriter, Carson Robison.

Chapter 3

PLAYBOYS
and Cowboys

As late as 1944, Columbia Records' one-man country music department, run by a dapper Englishman named Arthur (Uncle Art) Satherley, was telling the *Saturday Evening Post*, "I would never think of hiring a Mississippi boy to play in a Texas band. Any Texan would know right off it was wrong."

Satherley knew what he was talking about. Like Ralph Peer, he was a roving producer, but whereas Peer spent only ten years on the road, Satherley traveled from coast to coast for twenty-five years. He recorded singing cowboys in Hollywood, western swing bands in Texas, Cajuns in Louisiana and east Texas, and hillbilly musicians in Nashville, Chicago, and elsewhere. He was absolutely right in saying that a Texas musician would not fit into a hillbilly band; in fact, the king of western swing, Bob Wills, famously remarked to *Time* magazine, "Please don't confuse us with none of them hillbilly outfits."

The Carter Family played in church halls, school auditoriums, tents, and at outdoor socials. Their music was for quiet enjoyment. Western swing was played in dancehalls and beer joints. It was for dancing and carousing. The Appalachian musicians took their cue from back-porch fiddlers and banjo pickers; western swing musicians took their cue from jazz, blues, and pop. The Carter Family's songs addressed sin in all its forms, but never without retribution in the final verse ("The program is morally good," stated their advertisements); western swing seemed to view sin as an inevitability that might as well be embraced. The roots of Bob Wills' music were as humble as the roots of the Carter

above Roy Rogers.
opposite Gene Autry: the hero in the white hat.

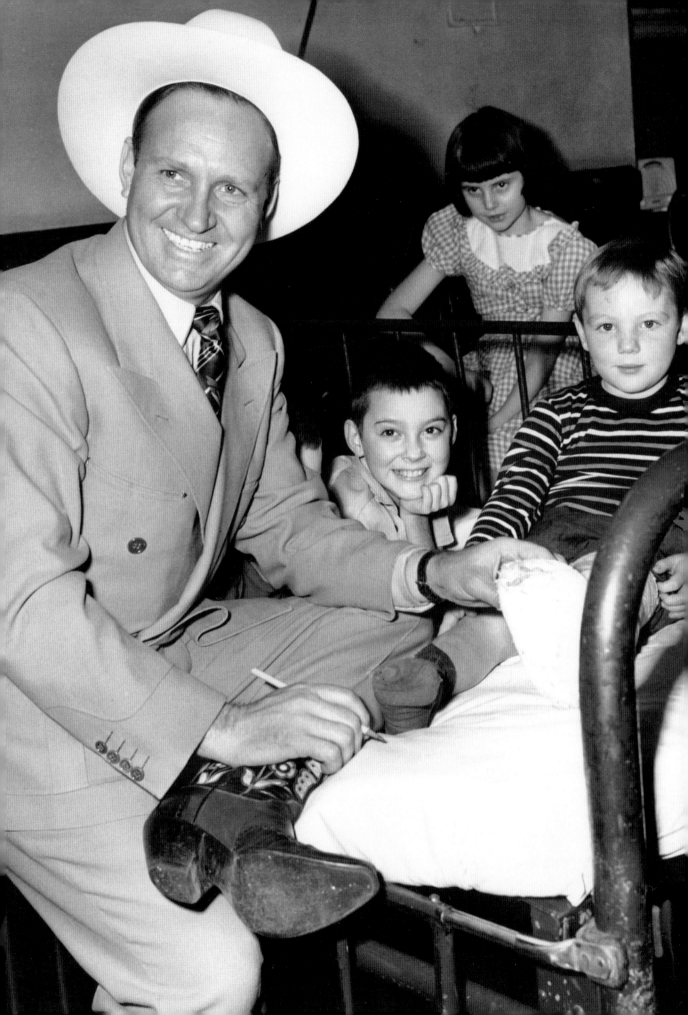

MILTON BROWN AND HIS BROWNIES
CRYSTAL SPRINGS
FORT WORTH TEXAS
SAM CUNNINGHAM MANAGER

Family's music. Wills' father played ranch parties and square dances in Texas. Wills, Sr. played the fiddle while young Bob played the mandolin. But Bob Wills, like most of the great innovators in American music, had astonishing catholicity of taste. He liked hillbilly string bands, vaudeville blues singers such as Bessie Smith, mainstream pop, jazz, and Mexican music. He was a farmer, a preacher, a medicine-show performer, and a barber. It all went into his music. The holy grails of western swing archaeologia are two recordings that Wills and his buddy Herman Arnspiger made in 1929. One of them was Bessie Smith's "Gulf Coast Blues" and the other was "Wills Breakdown." Perhaps in those two sides we would have heard the genesis of western swing, or perhaps we would have heard the reasons that Brunswick Records chose not to release them.

Wills was in a band called the Light Crust Doughboys with Milton Brown, and the two later had a good-natured rivalry. Brown did as much as, perhaps more than, Wills to codify the new music. He loved New Orleans jazz and minstrelsy, and almost certainly broadened Wills' musical palette.

Wills was an engaging singer, but not an especially good one; Brown was an excellent singer, who understood what the jazz singers understood. Like fellow white Texan Jack Teagarden, he laid back at any tempo, and sang with wonderfully detached irony. His band was top-notch, and featured a steel guitarist, Bob Dunn, whose phrasing was jagged, almost psychotic. Dunn was the first country musician to play the electrified steel guitar rather than the unamplified Hawaiian slide guitar, and he seems intoxicated with its potential. Finally, the guitar could drown out any other instrument. Milton Brown's Musical Brownies played music of great sophistication and charm, and might have gone a long way had Brown not perished in a 1936 car wreck alongside his sixteen-year-old girlfriend.

Swing music took off after the repeal of Prohibition in 1933. Western swing is generally reckoned to date from Milton Brown's 1934 sessions. Swing and western swing rose in tandem, and fell in tandem. Western swing was a regional phenomenon. The region was Texas and Oklahoma, and anywhere Texans and Oklahomans migrated, notably California. Milton Brown's Musical Brownies and Bob Wills' Texas Playboys were preeminent, but many other bands played this new jumped-up fiddle band music. In Tommy Duncan, Wills found a vocalist the equal of Milton Brown. Duncan sang with the same unflappability, and the same laconic drawl that bordered on sleaziness. He often sounded half-tanked, but his sense of time was impeccable. He toyed with the beat, came in late or early, but always finished precisely where he should.

Columbia Records signed Bob Wills and the Texas Playboys in 1935, and for the next twelve years he was one of the label's biggest stars. He recorded around 140 songs for the label, including many that still form the core of the western swing canon: "San Antonio Rose," "Spanish Two Step," "Maiden's Prayer," "Steel Guitar Rag," "Take Me Back to Tulsa," and "Stay a Little Longer." Two of Tommy Duncan's songs also became big hits: "Time Changes Everything" and "Bubbles in My Beer." Wills rarely sang on his records, and didn't even play fiddle very often, but his presence loomed over every session. He'd do his little asides while Duncan sang, he'd introduce the soloists, and he'd cut loose with his trademark "aaah-hah" whenever he felt like it. As trumpeter Alex Brashear lit into his solo on "Hang Your Head in Shame," Wills says, "Ahhh, here's a man after my heart…with a razor." On a couple of occasions, Wills was drunk at session time, so the band recorded without him, and the results were mundane. Wills added an intangible spark to every session. Many of his best-known numbers were orchestrated Texas fiddle tunes. He tried for ever-increasing sophistication, but his audience always brought him back to the fiddle tunes. He was never allowed to get too far above his raisin'. He was never allowed to get too far east of the Mississippi, either. Western swing remained truly

below Bob Wills with Tommy Duncan.

western. Wills appeared on *The Grand Ole Opry* just twice—in 1944 and 1948. Memories of those dates vary, but the fact remains that he never became a regular. Merle Haggard met Bob Wills in his later years and remembers Wills referring disparagingly to "east of the River musicians." "They just don't kick it out," Wills told him.

The swing era was over by 1950, and the western swing era followed close behind. Television meant that the dancehall wasn't the focus of everyone's life anymore. Wills had one last monumental hit, "Faded Love." It too was an orchestrated fiddle tune with lyrics newly added, and in Wills' hands it became a haunting, almost Celtic lament. Coming when it did, it not only echoed the vastness and loneliness of west Texas,

but almost seemed a requiem for the era just passed. Twenty years later, it became a recurring motif in Peter Bogdanovich's *Last Picture Show*, once again capturing the isolation and claustrophobia of small-town Texas.

Bob Wills somehow kept a band together through the rock 'n' roll era and beyond, and became a living cultural icon, while others took his sound in new directions. Hank Thompson's Brazos Valley Boys had the look of a western swing band, and Thompson's heart certainly remained in that era, but no one could mistake his big hits, such as "Wild Side of Life" and "Rub-a-Dub-Dub," for western swing. The real future of western swing was in the past. Revivalists such as Asleep at the Wheel kept the sound alive. Bigger names, such as George Strait, clearly loved the music and brought vestiges of it to their own sound. Some of Strait's hits, such as "Does Fort Worth Ever Cross Your Mind?", "Ace in the Hole," or "All My Ex's Live in Texas," could have been Playboy songs—pretty good ones at that.

Western music, otherwise known as cowboy songs, had very little in common with western swing. Perhaps more than any other form of country music, the original cowboy songs were English in origin. Folk songs, poems, and music-hall songs from the old country were rewritten to reflect the western experience. One of the best-known western songs, "The Streets of Laredo," was adapted from an eighteenth-century British broadside, "The Unfortunate Rake," and another well-known western song, "Sweet Betsy from Pike," came from an early Victorian music-hall number, "Villikins and His Dinah."

Cowboy music went through several distinct phases, mirroring the development of country music itself. Cowboy records became popular from the mid-1920s onward, and some of the original songs, such as "When the Work's All Done This Fall," became over-familiar. Others, such as "The Whorehouse Bells Were Ringing," didn't fit the freshly sanitized image of the cowpoke, so the new cowboy songs reformulated the west into an imaginary Eden, transforming the grim, hardscrabble reality of the cowboy's life into one-act morality plays. Tin Pan Alley got in on the act. "The Last Roundup" became the best-selling song of 1933 and made unlikely cowpokes out of Bing Crosby and Italian-Canadian big band leader Guy Lombardo. The 1935 hit "Take Me Back to My Boots and Saddles" was written by three New Yorkers who rarely ventured west of the Hudson River. They began it over tea one afternoon in the penthouse garden of New York's Hotel Olcott. No one seems to have asked the diminishing number of real cowboys what they made of this New York take on their life.

Tin Pan Alley was cranking out cowboy songs because Hollywood was cranking out cowboy movies. The biggest country music star from Jimmie Rodgers' death in 1933 to the end of the Second World War was Gene Autry. Starting as a Rodgers disciple, Autry cut smutty blues and covered Rodgers' hits for dimestore labels until he got lucky with the sentimental classic "That Silver Haired Daddy of Mine" in 1931. He still wasn't a cowboy singer, but he'd been signed to Columbia Records (or ARC, as it was known in those days) by Art Satherley, who'd arrived in the United States from England entranced by cowboys and all things western. Under Satherley's guidance, Autry concentrated on western songs and used his radio show on Chicago's powerhouse station, WLS, to build his new image. In 1934, he left for Hollywood because he'd landed a part in a Ken Maynard movie. Maynard is generally reckoned to be the first

left The Sons of the Pioneers with Roy Rogers (front, right).

singing cowboy, but Autry was the first singing cowboy star. Autry was just what the country needed during the Depression. He sang in a smooth, reassuring baritone, and his simple downhome goodness triumphed in movie after movie. In 1941, the Oklahoma town of Berwyn changed its name to Gene Autry, testifying to the singer's iconic power during the Depression and war years. Autry was no simple cowpoke, though. He had a good ear for a song, and recruited Fred Rose, later one of the founding fathers of the Nashville music business, as his in-house songwriter. Rose wrote several of Autry's biggest hits, but he didn't write his theme song, "Back in the Saddle Again," nor did he write "South of the Border," which was presented to Autry on a tour of England. "How two Englishmen [Michael Carr and Jimmy Kennedy] could write a song about a country they had never seen for a movie cowboy they had never met is a question I wish I could answer," Autry wrote in his autobiography. Such was the mythic power of the west during those interwar years.

Every Hollywood studio had a singing cowboy and nearly every radio station had an on-air singing cowboy, so the demand for material was intense. The most gifted writer of new western music was one of the original Sons of the Pioneers, Bob Nolan. Roy Rogers created the Sons of the Pioneers, and more or less invented western harmony singing in the process. Born in Cincinnati, Ohio, Rogers migrated west with his family, and the boom in western songs gave him the idea of a western harmony group. A newspaper ad yielded Bob Nolan, and the original trio was rounded out by Tim Spencer. These three non-westerners created the most original sound in western music, the "block harmony" style, melting three voices into one. They rehearsed endlessly (a trio yodel is no easy feat), and Nolan began writing songs such as "Tumbling Tumbleweeds," "Way Out There," and "Cool Water," which brought a modern sensibility, bordering on melancholy, to the cowboy song. Rogers soon left for a career in motion pictures, but the Sons of the Pioneers (albeit with no original members) remain an ongoing franchise. The west in Nolan's songs was nine parts myth to one part reality, but the myth began exercising an ever more powerful fascination as the real west slowly disappeared.

The cowboy made a comeback on the small screen starting with *Hopalong Cassidy* in 1949, and many of the television western theme songs did good business. There was another brief vogue for cowboy songs after Marty Robbins scored the biggest hit of 1960 with "El Paso," but western music had little influence on the course of country music from the end of the Depression. Ironically, though, *Billboard* magazine bracketed the two together in 1956 as "Country & Western," and the term stuck for decades, long after *Billboard* had dropped it.

ARE YOU ALL READY
FOR THE BIG WORLD'S SERIES
TUNE IN WITH A **RADIOLA**
Prices from $19⁴⁵ to $575⁰⁰
Complete Stock of Tubes & Batteries.

Chapter 4

TIN PAN VALLEY
Comes of Age

As Tin Pan Alley cranked out western songs, and as folk ballads, once handed down within families, now had little copyright notices appended to them, it was clear that country music and business had become entwined, and would remain so. The story of country music now begins to unfold against a background of broader developments in the music industry. Country music was now a commodity.

Just as new western songs were needed a few years after the first western recordings, so new country songs were needed just a few years after the first country recordings. When Ralph Peer exerted pressure upon his artists to write or acquire new material that he could publish, his motives weren't entirely selfish. Most recording was still done for flat fees, so Peer felt that writing the songs would give the artist, as well as himself, some profit participation.

In 1932, just seven years after discovering the Carter Family and Jimmie Rodgers, Peer left RCA Victor to concentrate on his publishing empire. He'd realized that music publishing might be the least sexy part of the business, but was by far the most profitable. Publishers collect a "mechanical" fee from the record label for every copy sold, an amount that has increased over the years from fractions of a cent to 8 cents per song. Publishers are fond of saying that artists come and go, but songs are forever. Even forgotten flip sides of hit singles make as much in mechanicals as the top side. Publishers usually split this revenue fifty/fifty with the songwriter.

above Rex Griffin.
opposite Radios in a Louisville, Kentucky store priced from $19.45 to $575.

Ever since the late nineteenth century, music publishing had been headquartered in New York, but the big publishers ignored country music and blues to the point that Peer and his fellow A&R men could acquire the publishing on almost everything they produced without much competition. The windfall income from these chance acquisitions could be enormous. In 1930, Peer (who also handled blues sessions for RCA Victor) recorded Gus Cannon's Jug Stompers singing "Walk Right In." Thirty-three years later, the song became a number one pop hit. After Peer quit, RCA's blues sessions were handled by a Chicago businessman named Lester Melrose. In 1946 Melrose recorded Arthur Crudup singing "That's All Right (Mama)" and casually acquired the publishing rights. Eight years later it became one of the most valuable copyrights in rock 'n' roll when Elvis Presley recorded it. The New York publishers' sniffy attitude toward blues and country cost them a fortune.

Performance income came no easier to country or blues songwriters. In 1909, Congress had decreed that music publishers should be paid for public performance of their copyrighted works, but collecting the payments was nearly impossible. In Europe, the problem was solved by performing rights societies collecting on behalf of publishers and composers. Giacomo Puccini toured the United States in 1910, and encouraged American composers and publishers to band together in a similar venture. The result was ASCAP (the American Society of Composers, Authors and Publishers). With ASCAP's background, it was hardly surprising that country songwriters were generally unwelcome, and blues songwriters doubly so. ASCAP also had a payment system based on an impossible-to-understand nine-point weighted

payment gauge that seemed to give most money to those who needed it least.

So country music required new songs, but there was barely any incentive to write them. Country sales were just a fraction of pop sales, and the A&R men would demand the music publishing rights and would then offer very low mechanical rates to the record labels. And membership in ASCAP was so hard to obtain that it was impossible to collect for broadcasts and performances.

right The hills are alive with the sound of music.

During the early part of the twentieth century, the newest songs in country music were generally pop songs that sounded like folk songs. Charles K. Harris's "After the Ball" was a classic ballad with a Kleenex climax that sounded as if it could have been written almost any time after 1700, but was actually written in 1892. William Shakespeare Hays, a little-known Kentuckian who died in 1907, wrote songs such as "Little Log Cabin in the Lane," "Mollie Darling," and "Jimmie Brown the Newsboy," all of which became country standards. The first quasi-professional country songwriter was Carson Robison, who cranked out songs for Vernon Dalhart in the wake of "The Prisoner's Song." Dalhart became a born-again hillbilly, and Robison wrote "event" songs and ballads for him, but quickly grew tired of surrendering 50 percent of the composer credit to Dalhart, and went out on his own in 1928. Robison hung around New York just enough for ASCAP to admit him in 1933. The Depression

provided plenty of grist for his peculiar talent ("Prosperity Is Just Around Which Corner?") and the war provided even more ("We're Gonna Have to Slap the Dirty Little Jap" and "Hitler's Last Letter to Hirohito"). After the war, he scored a big hit with "Life Gets Tee-Jus, Don't It," and, shortly before his death in 1957, he recorded "Rockin' and Rollin' with Grandma." He'd stayed on top of every trend in country music from event ballads to rockabilly.

During the 1920s and 1930s, the onus was upon the artists to find material. A. P. Carter would disappear for weeks at a time on song-scouting trips, and Jimmie Rodgers persuaded his sister-in-law Elsie McWilliams to set aside her straitlaced background and write songs such as "Everybody

opposite Cindy Walker.
below Carson Robison.

Does It in Hawaii." In general, if the artist's name is bracketed with someone else in the composer credit, it's a good indication that the artist had no hand in the composition, and that the songwriter had reluctantly decided that 50 percent of something beat 100 percent of nothing. Vernon Dalhart had demanded a half share, as did Jimmie Rodgers and Gene Autry. The tradition was still going strong into the 1950s and beyond. Nashville songwriters would joke bitterly among themselves that country star Webb Pierce had a rubber stamp saying "and Webb Pierce."

It wasn't until the 1940s that country songwriting became a viable profession. It happened so quickly that you can almost put a date on it: February 15, 1940. That day, Broadcast Music Inc. (BMI) was launched. Back in 1932, ASCAP had negotiated fees for radio performances with the National Association of Broadcasters (NAB), but in 1939 ASCAP decided to go for a much bigger piece of the pie, figuring that radio needed its songs and would capitulate. Instead, the NAB persuaded the station owners to pledge 50 percent of their ASCAP fees to the formation of a new performing rights society, Broadcast Music Inc. Just days after BMI was launched, ASCAP called for a two-fold increase in licensing fees, so the NAB promptly boycotted ASCAP-protected works. Some major music publishers switched allegiance to BMI, and others, such as Peer, launched BMI affiliates.

The dispute lasted ten months and ended when ASCAP settled for one-third of its original demand. By then, BMI was up and running, and acquiring songs in a hurry. The biggest source of copyrights lay in the areas that ASCAP had pointedly ignored: country, jazz, and blues. And so country music came in from the cold. It would have been better if the right thing had happened for the right reason, but the fact is

that it happened. Country songs, such as "You Are My Sunshine" and "Pistol Packin' Mama," became huge pop hits. Country songwriting suddenly became a career option.

The first really successful country songwriter was Cindy Walker. She set out for Hollywood in 1941 with a briefcase full of songs. Nashville didn't enter her mind because there were no music publishers there in 1941. She had the idea of becoming a performer, even made some records, but soon realized that she was better suited to songwriting. She pitched songs to Bing Crosby, but really hit her stride writing for Bob Wills. Among her fifty-plus songs for Wills were "Bubbles in My Beer," "You're

from Texas," and the eerie "Dusty Skies." The last of these was ostensibly about a cattle drive, but when Wills' vocalist Tommy Duncan sings "all of the grass and water's gone/We'll have to keep movin' on," it seemed less about a cowboy losing his herd than about poor Okie farmers losing their land. Walker proved supremely adaptable, writing love songs for Eddy Arnold, beerjoint anthems for Ernest Tubb, and rock 'n' roll for Roy Orbison. One of her last major hits, "Distant Drums," blurred the tonality between past and present, much as "Dusty Skies" had done. Ostensibly set during a past conflict, it came at the dawn of the Vietnam war.

Very few early country songwriters delved deep into personal experience. Perhaps it was the legacy of traditional story songs told in the third person, perhaps it was thought unbecoming in that buttoned-up era. One of the earliest writers to jettison sentimentality and draw on personal feelings was Rex Griffin. Almost forgotten these days, Griffin bared his soul in song after song through the late years of the Depression, and left a small, heartbreaking legacy. Griffin was signed to Decca Records as a Jimmie Rodgers soundalike two years after the Blue Yodeler's death, but he wrote a song greater than any Rodgers ever wrote or acquired. Titled "The Last Letter," it was the suicide note of an older man besotted with a younger woman.

Why do you treat me as if I were only a friend?
What have I done to make you so different and cold?
Sometimes I wonder if you'll be contented again.
Will you be happy when you are withered and old?

I cannot offer you diamonds and mansions so fine.
I cannot offer you clothes that your young body craves.
But if you'll say that you long to forever be mine
Think of the heartaches, the tears, and the sorrows
*   you'll save.*

When you are lonely and tired of another man's gold,
When you are weary, remember this letter, my own,
Don't try to answer though I'll suffer anguish untold
If you don't love me I wish you would leave me alone.

While I am writing this letter, I think of the past
And of the promises that you are breaking so free,
But to this old world I'll soon say my farewell at last,
I will be gone when you read this last letter from me.

Griffin, like Jimmie Rodgers and Tommy Duncan, sang with a slightly drunken slur, but Griffin's vocals were further distorted by a speech impediment that made "from" come out as "fwom." The impediment made him sound all the more vulnerable. Griffin went on to write "Everybody's Trying to Be My Baby" that Carl Perkins adapted and the Beatles later recorded. He also wrote "Just Call Me Lonesome," one of the great country songs of the 1950s, but by the time Eddy Arnold recorded it in 1955, Griffin was a sick man. He moved to New Orleans and drank up the proceeds. Like his idol, Jimmie Rodgers, he contracted tuberculosis and died young.

Back in 1939, Griffin recorded a vaudeville number, "Lovesick Blues." He probably remembered a blackface performer, Emmett Miller, singing it in the 1920s, but he changed the song around, making one of the verses into the chorus and the chorus into a verse. In 1942, another young Alabama hillbilly singer, Hank Williams, began singing "The Last Letter" on his radio show, and then, seven years later, Williams made Rex Griffin's arrangement of "Lovesick Blues" into his breakthrough hit.

opposite Rex Griffin.

Chapter 5

There's a Little NIGHTSPOT *on the Outskirts of Town...*

"The program is morally good," the Carter Family assured their audiences, and so the good people came to little schoolhouses, small-town auditoriums, and church halls. Meanwhile, Jimmie Rodgers was singing about his "Rough and Rowdy Ways" and about everybody doing it in Hawaii.

above Jimmie Davis with Red Foley (left) and Gene Autry (center).
opposite Ernest Tubb and the Texas Troubadours bring traffic to a halt in Nashville, 1944. Whitey Ford (left), the Duke of Paducah, is the master of ceremonies.

Rodgers wasn't playing little church halls in Appalachia; he was working concert tours across the country. While the Carters' music led eventually to bluegrass, many more musicians took their cue from Rodgers and played rough and rowdy music in rough and rowdy, out-of-the-way places.

The end of Prohibition in 1933 set the stage for a huge increase in the number of bars. They were usually just outside the city limits, where they wouldn't attract the attention of better-manned, better-equipped city police forces. Taxes were lower, land was cheaper, and country folk wouldn't have to drive all the way downtown. They were called "jukejoints" or "beerjoints" or just "joints." Often, they were called "honky-tonks," though no one really knows where the name came from. "Honky-tonk" has the reduplicative quality of African-American words, such as "boogie-woogie." Writer Nick Tosches found mention of a "honk-a-tonk" in the 1890s, and there were blues records with "honky-tonk" in the title back in the 1920s. Two country musicians, Al Dexter and Jimmie Davis, recorded different songs called "Honky Tonk Blues" in 1936 and 1937 respectively, and didn't feel the need to explain what a honky-tonk was, so it must have crept into impolite white

society by then. Davis had started as a Jimmie Rodgers disciple, and in his recording of "Honky Tonk Blues" you can hear the transition between Rodgers' restraint and the emerging honky-tonk sound. The backbeat is heavier and the piano is to the fore. The guitar plays chunky full chords, underscoring the beat. It was, in many ways, stripped-down western swing music without the sophistication.

By the time Jimmie Davis recorded "Honky Tonk Blues," his honky-tonkin' days were almost behind him. He'd started his career singing smutty blues songs, smuttier than anything Jimmie Rodgers ever sang. "Red Nightgown Blues," "She's a Hum-Dum-Dinger from Dingersville," "Tom Cat and Pussy Blues," and many others were lovely performances, their rich innuendo underscored by a slide guitar. Davis then became a criminal court clerk in

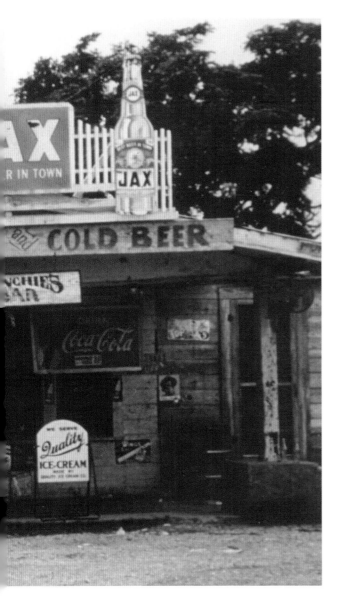

for Commissioner of Public Safety and then, in 1944, for Governor of Louisiana. His opponents tried to dredge up the smutty blues records, but they only enhanced his popularity. He would make no more honky-tonkin' records, though.

Al Dexter owned a bar in the Texas oilfields. Honky-tonks had sprouted up there long before the end of Prohibition, and one night Dexter saw a barroom fight that provided the inspiration for his epochal hit "Pistol Packin' Mama." Its opening line, "Drinking beer in a cabaret," left no doubt about its origins. Producer Art Satherley didn't care for it, but the insistent rhythm persuaded him to release it anyway. *Life* magazine hated it: "It is naive, folksy, and almost completely devoid of meaning. Its melody line is simple, its lyric rowdy, and of course monotonously tautological." But it became a wartime sensation, bigger even than "You Are My Sunshine." Copies were rationed because 78 rpm records were pressed on a shellac-based compound, and shellac was required for munitions. Jukebox operators were paying up to $10 for a copy. Bing Crosby and the Andrews Sisters performed their strange alchemy on it. Just as the Andrews Sisters deracinated a calypso about prostitution, "Rum and Coca Cola," so "Pistol Packin' Mama" was sung with such levity that you'd almost never know that it was about a cross-eyed oil field worker being shot by his wife near Turnertown, Texas. But honky-tonk music had arrived. When *Billboard* magazine launched its first country chart on January 1, 1944, "Pistol Packin' Mama" was still number one.

Several factors coalesced here. Country boys were leaving the country. Even before the United States entered the war in 1941, munitions plants were going full tilt, and before then there was plenty of work in the oilfields and auto plants. It was backbreaking, dehumanized work, and honky-

Shreveport, Louisiana, where he acquired a song, "Nobody's Darlin' but Mine," from a hillbilly singer named Bill Nettles, who found himself on the other side of the bars. In 1940, Davis acquired "You Are My Sunshine" in more mysterious circumstances. Until his death, he claimed to have written it (all evidence to the contrary), but he certainly copyrighted, recorded, and popularized it. Meanwhile, he developed a taste for public office, running first

tonk music was the sound of the displaced Southerner with a little change in his pocket. It was the sound of the hillbilly in the land of the wind chill factor, or the Okie in the vast melting pot of southern California, or the Texas farm boy working the rigs in the Permian oil basin. For every good-timing honky-tonk song, there was another, darker one. It was music that reeked of stale beer funk, sweat, and smoke, and it was music that had to be played loud in order to be heard. The electric guitar and electric steel guitar (both 1930s' innovations) came to the fore alongside the piano and drums. Mandolins, dulcimers, and banjos stayed home.

Two artists defined 1940s' honky-tonk music: Floyd Tillman and Ernest Tubb. Shortly before Tillman made his first records under his own name in 1939, he wrote one of the great honky-tonk anthems, "It Makes No Difference Now." It was yet another song that Jimmie Davis bought (although

unlike others on the losing end of Davis's deals, Tillman got his song back). In sentimental parlor ballads, such as "After the Ball," a man lives alone his entire life because he thought he'd seen his fiancée with another man. "It Makes No Difference Now" was almost diametrically opposite. Its message was quite blunt: "So you're leaving? Screw you!" Tillman went on to write "Slipping Around," the first cheating song that neither moralized nor condemned, but it was his vocal style that really marked him out as a honky-tonk singer. His first records were sung straight, but by the mid-1940s he was singing as if his world were viewed through the bottom of a shot glass. He slurred words, broke meter, and bent notes in a manner that Willie Nelson would later emulate. "This Cold War with You" was quint-essential Floyd Tillman in its brutal unsentimentality.

The sun goes down and finds me sad and blue
Leaving another night of this cold war with you
For you won't speak and I won't speak, it's true
Two stubborn people with a cold war to go through.

Ernest Tubb sang in a rough-hewn baritone and couldn't hold a note to save his life, but his records oozed believability. His life was a little catechism in what it meant to be a country star. He took his music to isolated hamlets and would stand outside the dance hall in bone-chilling cold or stifling heat until every last autograph had been signed, every last hand shaken, every last photo snapped.

Ernest Tubb grew up in awe of Jimmie Rodgers, and even won Mrs. Rodgers' personal endorsement and the right to play the Blue Yodeler's guitar. His first records were for Rodgers' label, RCA Victor, but by 1940, he was off Victor and living in San Angelo, Texas. He stopped yodeling, brought the electric guitar into his line-up, and began writing songs that owed a less obvious debt to his mentor. By the spring of 1941, he was signed to Decca, but was on the point of being dropped. His wife, Elaine, had left him, and he was pacing back and forth in his rooming house one night when "Walking the Floor Over You" came to him. Around the same time, he wrote another sour valentine to Elaine, "Mean Mama Blues." Elaine's problems were compounded by the death of their second son. A beer case in her car had come loose at a sudden stop, crushing the child, a tragedy that Tubb etched memorably into a song, "Our Baby's Book." He might have lost the sympathy vote if he had mentioned the cause of the child's death, but "Our Baby's Book" was released at a time when infant mortality was higher, and touched many hearts. So, for very different reasons, did "Walking the Floor Over You" and "Mean Mama Blues."

Tubb came into his own during the war years with hits such as "Soldier's Last Letter," "Rainbow at Midnight," and "It's Been So Long, Darling."

above Ernest Tubb at a 1960s' recording session.

The last of these captured the mix of trepidation and longing as returning servicemen neared home after years away. Tubb became the voice of a generation, and one of the first country stars to have cross-country appeal (*Billboard* pegged his royalties for the first six months of 1947 at an astonishing $50,000). He joined *The Grand Ole Opry* and moved to Nashville in 1943. By the 1950s, he was an institution. Ol' E. T.

Honky-tonk music has gone in and out of vogue, but in times of crisis country music has often retreated to its honky-tonk roots. Drinking songs, cheatin' songs, and beerhall shuffles were the white man's blues. And, like the blues, honky-tonk music is profoundly adult music. Whenever country music chases the youth dollar, its honky-tonk roots are the first to go, but whenever it tries to rediscover its greatness and uniqueness, honky-tonk reappears.

Chapter 6

BLUEGRASS:
Water from an Ancient Well

The one area of country music where electrified instruments have never been welcome is bluegrass. Inherently reactionary on many levels, bluegrass is assumed to be ancient music, but the music we know as bluegrass stems from the mid-1940s, and was as revolutionary as it was reactionary. One figure still towers over it: Bill Monroe.

In bluegrass as Monroe formulated it, mountain music met square-dance tunes, Victorian parlor songs, blues, jazz, and hymnody. It was fierce, insurgent music, reflecting the personality of its originator. Very few artists can claim to have invented an entire musical genre, and even those who insist that Bill Monroe didn't invent bluegrass have to admit that it probably wouldn't exist as we know it without him.

Bill Monroe was born in rural west Kentucky near the settlement of Rosine, the youngest of eight children. His parents were middle-aged when he was born, and dead by the time he was sixteen. Monroe had a bad squint, and grew up with a sense of apartness that resonated throughout his music. After his parents' death, he spent a year or two with his mother's brother, Pendleton Vandiver, whom he later immortalized in "Uncle Pen." As Monroe relates in the song, Uncle Pen was a fiddle player who played socials around Rosine, but he too was dead by the time Monroe was nineteen. Like many of his generation, Monroe went north to join his brothers in the auto plants and related industries, but before long they were playing to homesick Southerners on the

above Bill Monroe—bluegrass patriarch.
opposite Bill Monroe—*Opry* newcomer.

right The classic band—Bill Monroe (at microphone) with Chubby Wise on his right and Flatt & Scruggs on his left.

shores of Lake Michigan. Moving on to the Carolinas, Bill and Charlie Monroe were sponsored on radio by Crazy Water Crystals (a Depression era tonic that claimed to cure diseases caused "by a sluggish system") and became local stars. RCA Victor signed them in 1936, and their first record, "What Would You Give in Exchange for Your Soul," became a huge hit in the southeast. In all, they recorded sixty songs. Many of them had been recorded previously, but the Monroes made songs such as "Nine Pound Hammer," "Roll on Buddy," "Roll in My Sweet Baby's Arms," and "New River Train" into standards.

The Monroes fought and eventually separated in 1938. Bill Monroe recorded two more sessions for RCA with his new group, now dubbed the Blue Grass Boys. In 1940, he recorded an electrifying version of Jimmie Rodgers' "Mule Skinner Blues." "The beat in my music started when I ran across 'Mule Skinner Blues,'" he said later. "We don't do it the way Jimmie Rodgers sang it. It's speeded up, and we moved it up to fit the fiddle." Monroe, in other words, transformed "Mule Skinner," just as Elvis Presley would later transform Monroe's "Blue Moon of Kentucky." "Mule Skinner Blues" was turbocharged string-band music, not yet bluegrass. Monroe played it at his *Grand Ole Opry* audition, and was told he had a job for life.

The *Opry* made Ernest Tubb and Roy Acuff into coast-to-coast stars, but Monroe's popularity remained localized in the South and southeast. He played *Opry* tent shows throughout that area, shows that became life-altering experiences for young musicians in the audience. The Blue Grass Boys were *that* good. Monroe brought a confrontational

intensity to his music. He sang high, going for nut-clenching notes, and rarely tried to make his music more accessible. His attitude was unapologetic: this is my music—take it or leave it. He'd become a fearsomely good mandolin player, very bluesy and very passionate, and, as with Louis Armstrong, there was a physicality about his playing. Many in country music at the time cherished showmanship above technical virtuosity, but Monroe demanded virtuosity of himself and his musicians, and encouraged competition within the band. He drew an analogy

with his favorite sport, baseball: everyone was on the same team, yet in competition with each other. Monroe also refused to play up to hillbilly stereotypes. He dressed his band in riding attire (jodhpurs and breeches), and ensured that they were always smart. "I think that was one of the gooder things Bill ever done," said Ralph Stanley. "Bill dressed neat and he wore a hat and he was always shaved and he was always neat. It means a lot in this, in any kind of music, to look good and have a good appearance before your audience of

followers." Through the war years, Monroe continued to add and subtract players. At one time or another, the Blue Grass Boys' line-up included accordion, jug, and harmonica. The classic bluegrass sound was close, but had yet to be codified.

In 1943, Columbia Records' Art Satherley poached Monroe away from RCA Victor. Monroe had been hoarding some good songs, and would sing some of his earliest Columbia recordings, such as "Footprints in the Snow," "Rocky Road Blues," and "Kentucky Waltz," for the remainder of his life.

In 1945, soon after the first Columbia session, he hired a new vocalist and guitarist, Lester Flatt, and later that year a young banjo player, Earl Scruggs, came into the group. The classic line-up was now complete. Scruggs played the banjo in a revolutionary way. Earlier banjo players brushed the strings or picked with two fingers, but Scruggs played a dextrous three-finger style that could be adapted to any tempo, and had the imagination to go anywhere Monroe sent him. Flatt & Scruggs spent less than three years with Bill Monroe, but the music they made together remains the benchmark for bluegrass music. The impact of their twenty-eight recordings was inestimable, and it was inevitable that others would work in this style.

Monroe, it must be said, was curmudgeonly in his dealings with others who played what he considered *his* music. Proprietorial to a fault, he refused to speak to former band members for years or sometimes decades. The story of his relationship with other bluegrass bands got off to an especially fractious start: he had rearranged an old folk song about a horse race, "Molly and Tenbrooks," and recorded it shortly before the American Federation of Musicians (angry that records seemed to be killing off live music) called a recording ban in 1948. Columbia Records hoarded material in anticipation of a long shutdown, but Monroe began playing "Molly and Tenbrooks" on *The Opry*. The Stanley Brothers copied his arrangement and recorded it for a small label that paid no attention to the union ban. Ralph Stanley has never quite been able to admit the extent to which Monroe influenced him. He insists that he didn't copy Earl Scruggs, and that they'd both learned the three-finger banjo

above Bill Monroe plays *The Grand Ole Opry*, 1966, with Richard Greene on fiddle.

technique from the same players, and he also says that he didn't think of himself as a bluegrass musician. "I was singing music long before bluegrass," he says. "I like bluegrass, but I think the difference is bluegrass is a little bit more polished, and got a little bit more of a beat to it than the type of singing that I do." The fact remained, though, that the Stanley Brothers learned how older songs could be reinterpreted by listening to Monroe, and several who knew the Stanley Brothers during this period say that whatever Monroe sang at *The Opry* on Saturday night would be in the Stanleys' repertoire by Monday.

Ralph Stanley's older brother, Carter, went on to become a truly great songwriter, and the Stanley Brothers became almost as influential as Monroe himself. They'd grown up in rural southwest Virginia, near the Carter Family's home town, and they'd learned many old Appalachian songs, such as "I'm a Man of Constant Sorrow" and "Pretty Polly," from their parents. The Stanleys were on the radio in Raleigh, North Carolina, when Columbia's Art Satherley flew from New York to sign them in 1948. Their work for Columbia and subsequently for Mercury, Starday, and King Records is almost entirely unblemished. Above all, it seemed to convey an almost unbearable sense of loss. "The Fields Have Turned Brown" was the story of a country boy who returns home after years away to find the old homeplace empty. "For years they've been dead," ran the tag line, "the fields have turned brown." The same theme was revisited in "Rank Stranger," perhaps the ghostliest song that the Stanley Brothers recorded. They seemed to gravitate to the dark places, and Ralph's soaring mountain tenor was arguably the most thrilling sound in bluegrass, reinforcing the umbilical link to the music's roots. The brothers adapted an old hymn, "O Come Angel

Band," into "Angel Band," and Carter wrote several songs that have become bluegrass classics, including "White Dove," "The Lonesome River," and "How Mountain Girls Can Love." The partnership ended on December 1, 1966 when Carter died of complications from alcoholism at the age of forty-one. Ralph, not yet forty, thought initially of retirement but went on to a solo career that, commercially at least, has eclipsed the Stanley Brothers. "I'd say, if anything after Carter passed away, I took it back a little farther," he said.

The Stanley Brothers began their recording career in late 1947, and early the following year Flatt & Scruggs left Monroe. Scruggs had handled some of Monroe's book-keeping, and thus had a very good idea of the benefits of leadership. They joined Mercury Records, which had been in business for just three years, and in December 1949 recorded perhaps the best-known bluegrass tune of

all time, "Foggy Mountain Breakdown." A disarmingly simple sixteen-bar banjo showcase, it was similar in some ways to Monroe's "Blue Grass Breakdown," but it had a drive and inexpressible magic that came from Scruggs' absolute mastery of his instrument. Nearly twenty years later, it became a recurring motif in the movie *Bonnie and Clyde*, and was a hit all over again.

Bluegrass had its first artistic flowering in the late 1940s and early 1950s at a time when it was seen as a subset of hillbilly music, and only after the onset of rock 'n' roll in the mid-1950s was the term "bluegrass" used to differentiate it from Nashville's commercial product. Ironically, "bluegrass" entered the country music lexicon just as the music itself seemed likely to die out. Virtually all bluegrass musicians on major labels lost their deals, and the decline of live radio further eroded the music's exposure. The music retreated. Smaller stations, smaller markets, smaller labels, smaller sales.

Salvation came from an unlikely source. The catalyst for the late 1950s' folk music boom was an old stringband song, "Tom Dooley." Ralph Peer had produced the original 1929 version by Grayson and Whitter (Grayson, incidentally, was the nephew of Colonel James Grayson, who had captured the song's subject, Tom Dula, in 1866). Several other artists sang it through the years, but in 1958 the Kingston Trio recorded it, and it became the best-selling record of the year. The folk music boom was under way. The Kingston Trio were pop musicians singing folk songs, but they sparked an interest in indigenous folk music, especially on campuses. Bluegrass wasn't really folk music, but that's how it was marketed. Alan Lomax wrote an article for *Esquire* magazine in October 1959 in which he

left Flatt & Scruggs.

right Lester Flatt (far right) on the road late in life with Marty Stuart (second from right).

memorably described bluegrass as "folk music with overdrive." Bluegrass was coming in from the cold. Radio airplay might be hard to come by but college bookers were calling. Then came festivals. The first bluegrass festival was held in 1960, and by the end of the decade they were proliferating. At last count, there were several hundred every year.

Flatt & Scruggs' career says much about the pressures felt by bluegrass musicians in the years after rock 'n' roll. Their late 1950s' syndicated television show was seen by millions in the southeast, and the duo eclipsed Bill Monroe to become the most popular bluegrass act. They made some folk-oriented albums and appeared at the Newport Folk Festival. Then, in 1962, they were chosen to sing "The Ballad of Jed Clampett," titling one of the most successful television shows of the 1960s, *The Beverly Hillbillies*. Flatt & Scruggs had hung onto their major label deal through the years, but now they were faced with the inescapable fact that faces all major label artists: sales are always projected up, never down. Flatt & Scruggs had been signed to Columbia Records in 1950 by Art Satherley (soon after Satherley's signing of the Stanley Brothers prompted the ever-aggrieved Monroe to leave). Satherley's assistant, another Englishman named Don Law, took over in 1952, producing Flatt & Scruggs until his own retirement in 1967. Like Satherley, Law truly loved mountain music, but his successor, Bob Johnston, had made his name producing Bob Dylan and wanted to make Flatt & Scruggs relevant. Scruggs' sons also wanted to take the act in new directions, and the result was some egregiously bad music, capped by a version of Dylan's "Rainy Day Women #12 and 35." "I got

nuthin' against Bob Die-lan," Flatt remarked later. "He just don't write our kind of music." And so Flatt & Scruggs split. Flatt went back to bluegrass music and eventually made peace with Monroe. Scruggs formed a revue with his sons, but retired in 1980.

Artists and audiences could be no further apart—politically, geographically, or socially—than bluegrass musicians and campus crowds. The older musicians didn't understand the campus crowds, but they understood gate receipts. Country star Marty Stuart began his career working as a mandolin player for Lester Flatt. "Lester became a rock star," said Stuart. "We started working college campuses a *lot*. The first show was Michigan State. Gram Parsons and Emmylou Harris opened for us. The Eagles were out touring with 'Desperado' then, and Bernie Leadon wanted to meet Lester. I remember sitting in with Gram and Emmy, and talking to Bernie and I got on the bus that night and thought, 'This is how music

should be. You can do it all. No boundaries.' Lester said, 'Aw, this ain't gonna amount to nuthin',' but it did. I don't really know what Lester thought about that crowd. He and Earl had played for a lot of hippies in the 1960s. It wasn't brand new to him. But Lester was a businessman."

Most of the younger musicians who came to bluegrass in the 1960s and beyond weren't content to play the old music in the old way. There were many attempts to merge bluegrass with other forms of music, some successful, most not. The technical proficiency of the younger groups usually fails to compensate for the dearth of mountain soul. The hauntedness and confrontational fierceness that informed early bluegrass evaporated. In Bill Monroe's hands, bluegrass was never pretty music, but in the hands of Alison Krauss and Nickel Creek it is. Krauss in particular should have alerted the major labels to the

potential and perhaps the future of bluegrass. A fiddle contest winner, she began recording in 1987, fusing bluegrass, folk, and contemporary songcraft, and her albums for the independent Rounder Records sold millions of copies.

Bluegrass has waxed and waned in popularity, but Bill Monroe, who died in 1996, didn't live long enough to witness the latest explosion in the music's popularity. Although often attributed to the hugely successful soundtrack recording *O Brother, Where Art Thou?*, bluegrass was already gaining in popularity before the album's release. Mainstream Nashville artists became born-again bluegrass artists, and in July 2002 *Billboard* magazine announced that it would start a bluegrass chart. In bluegrass, there was once an old joke that the least commonly heard phrase in the English language was "That's the banjo player's Porsche." Suddenly the Porsche was very attainable.

Chapter 7

Tonight, Live from NASHVILLE, Tennessee...

As late as the 1940s, there were few country music dee-jays; in fact, few country records were even licensed for airplay. Inasmuch as country music was on-air, it was almost always "live." The American Federation of Musicians preferred it that way, believing that records were killing off live performances.

The musicians also preferred it that way because they stood little chance of getting paid for record airplay, and even though the stations usually paid little or nothing, a radio show could be used to advertise upcoming shows and sell songbooks. Country music was usually packaged for radio in the form of "live" fifteen-minute early morning shows and weekend barn dances.

The Grand Ole Opry is the most famous radio barn dance (and now one of the few remaining), but it wasn't the first. On the night of January 4, 1923, WBAP in Fort Worth, Texas, programmed ninety minutes of square-dance music by a Confederate war veteran, Captain M. J. Bonner, who sawed away at his fiddle to the accompaniment of an Hawaiian band. No other performer in WBAP's short history elicited as many telegrams and letters, so the station came up with the idea of a radio barn dance.

Much the same thing happened in Nashville. On November 28, 1925, Uncle Jimmy Thompson, then aged 77, came to newly launched WSM with his fiddle and his niece, played a program of fiddle tunes, and the station was deluged with calls, letters, and telegrams. WSM's owners, the National Life Insurance Company, was keen to reach rural areas and immediately okayed a radio barn

above DeFord Bailey.
opposite *The Opry* stage.

dance. Dubbed the *WSM Barn Dance*, it was juggled around various timeslots until 1927, when it became a fixture on Saturday night. Uncle Jimmy was a bit of a problem. He turned up drunk every now and again, and soon found what other performers on the show would find: he could make much more money elsewhere on Saturday night.

WSM wasn't a country station. Its broadcast day was a mosaic of society doings, drama, news, and music. Some of the music came from network feeds, and some was generated locally. One night, WSM manager, George D. Hay, had to segue from an opera coming in on the network feed to *WSM's Barn Dance*, and told the listeners to get ready for some "grand old op'ra." The name stuck, but just as WSM was not an all-country station so *The Opry* was not an all-country show. There were comedians (some of them still in blackface), pop and sacred quartets, dancers, and a black harmonica player named DeFord Bailey. *The Opry*'s success spurred WSM to begin programming country musicians "live" on-air during the early morning hours, but for many years the station was best known for its orchestra, which included pianist-arranger Owen Bradley, later an architect of the Nashville Sound. WSM's schedule also featured orchestra leader Francis Craig, who went on to score one of the biggest pop hits of all time, "Near You."

There were hundreds, perhaps thousands, of radio barn dances on big and small stations. Local station owners were legendarily eccentric, and often bought stations to conduct quixotic crusades (Roy Orbison began his career playing country music on KVWC in Vernon, Texas, when KVWC was an acronym for Keep Vernon Women Clean). A performer trying to carve out a career in country

left Lined up to see *The Grand Ole Opry.*

opposite Pee Wee King (left) puts the finishing touches to "Tennessee Waltz" with Redd Stewart.

music would typically start at a small-market radio barn dance. If he or she became popular, a sponsor would offer an early morning radio show, which might lead to a larger-market radio barn dance. Artists would work a city until they'd "played it out," then move on. The ultimate goal was to join one of the premier radio barn dances, such as WLS's *National Barn Dance* in Chicago, WLW's *Boone County Jamboree* (later known as *The Midwestern Hayride*) in Cincinnati, the *Renfro Valley Barn Dance* (also in Cincinnati), KRLD's *Big "D" Jamboree* in Dallas, KWKH's *Louisiana Hayride* in Shreveport, or Nashville's *Grand Ole Opry*. The biggest stations broadcast with 50,000 watts, blanketing most of the country after dark, and servicing such huge areas that it was almost impossible to play them out.

Today, the goal of every country singer is to get on record, but records barely figured into the equation in the 1920s, 1930s, and 1940s. RCA Victor's standard royalty rate for most of its country records was one-eighth of a cent per side sold, so if a record sold 10,000 copies, the performer would net $25, and few records sold as many as 10,000 copies. The goal was to join a major market barn dance, and of those *The Grand Ole Opry* slowly became preeminent. WSM's radio director, George D. Hay, enforced strict inverted snobbery, insisting on group names such as the Gully Jumpers, the Fruit Jar Drinkers, and the Dixie Clodhoppers. Straw bales piled around the stage and outhouse jokes confirmed his intention. In 1930, Harry Stone took over from Hay as program director, leaving Hay as the announcer. Stone hired an out-of-work concert violinist, Vito Pelletieri, to work on scheduling, and they divided the show into sponsored timeslots,

giving each timeslot its own star. The new structure ensured that no artist would become more popular than the show.

WSM then set up the Artist Service Bureau to organize tours throughout the station's huge listening area, and helped negotiate recording contracts. By the close of the 1930s, *The Opry* featured three relatively new stars, Roy Acuff, Bill Monroe, and a Polish accordionist named Julius Kuczynski, who had experienced a conversion to country music after working some shows with Gene Autry. Renamed Pee Wee King, Kuczynski went on to cowrite "Tennessee Waltz." The new roster's popularity persuaded WSM's management to go after a network timeslot. WSM was affiliated with the NBC radio network, and in October 1939, WSM manager Jack Stapp persuaded the network to pick up half an hour of *The Opry*. Prince Albert Tobacco sponsored the networked portion, and Roy Acuff was chosen as host. Country music had finally realized its quest for prime-time. The coast-to-coast exposure made *The Opry* the top radio barn dance, and in 1940 several cast members journeyed to Hollywood to make a movie called *The Grand Ole Opry*.

The networked Prince Albert portion of *The Opry* made Roy Acuff into a national star. Born on a tenant farm near Knoxville, Tennessee, he grew up in the foothills of the Smoky Mountains. A baseball career seemed likely until he was sidelined by a debilitating bout of sunstroke. During the layoff, he honed his skill on the fiddle, and formed a band called the Crazy Tennesseans. Later in life, Acuff tried to gloss over this period, but the Crazy Tennesseans put on a vaudeville show that included several smutty songs. Two of them, "When Lulu's Gone" (better known as "Bang, Bang Lulu") and "Doin' It the Old Fashioned Way," made their way onto disc. Acuff then paid 50 cents to someone he

remembered only as "Charlie" for a song called "Great Speckle [sic] Bird." In the Book of Jeremiah, the speckled bird was a metaphor for the Church assailed by evil ("Mine heritage is unto me as a speckled bird, the birds round about are against her"). It was a strange, elliptical song, unusually rich in metaphor for a country song. The melody had probably crossed from the British Isles; in fact, the same melody had already been used by the Carter Family on "I'm Thinking Tonight of My Blue Eyes" and would later be adapted into "The Wild Side of Life" and "It Wasn't God Who Made Honky Tonk Angels." Acuff performed "The Great Speckle Bird" on *The Grand Ole Opry* on February 5, 1938, and the response led to an invitation to join the cast. Once on *The Opry*, Acuff dropped the smutty songs, and the Crazy Tennesseans became the not-so-crazy Smoky Mountain Boys.

Acuff found several songs that became his signature pieces. The structure of *The Opry* was such that he would rarely have time to sing more

than two or three songs, so almost every week the 2500 attendees at *The Opry* house, together with 10 million listening in, could count on Acuff singing "Great Speckle Bird," "Night Train to Memphis," "The Precious Jewel," "Wabash Cannonball," "Fireball Mail," or "Death on the Highway." The last of these was quintessential Acuff. It was a grisly number, originally titled "Didn't Hear Nobody Pray," but Acuff retitled it and claimed it as his own. "There was whiskey and blood together, mixed with glass where they lay …I heard the groans of the dying, but I didn't hear nobody pray." The sinners were so lost in sin they couldn't even pray at the last, thus redeeming their poor wicked souls. Acuff sang in a full-throated, emotional style that sounded good crackling through the ether on Saturday night. He hired a Dobro player, and the Dobro's tremulous sound perfectly echoed his style. Acuff appeared in movies, toured the country, and twice ran for Governor of Tennessee. He was so popular during the war years that the Army reckoned he outranked Sinatra, and he reportedly earned an astonishing $200,000 in 1942. In Acuff's hands, country music was just that: music for the country people of the South and southeast. He provided a link between ancient stringband music and the modern era, and epitomized country music's innate cultural and political conservatism.

Throughout the 1940s, *The Grand Ole Opry* was hugely popular. The show never paid more than "scale" (the absolute minimum mandated by the American Federation of Musicians for a radio appearance), and demanded that its stars appear almost every Saturday night. No matter where they were in the nation, they had to get back to Nashville

above Roy Acuff (right) hands over the networked portion of *The Grand Ole Opry* to Red Foley.
opposite Roy Acuff backstage with Ricky Skaggs.

or risk dismissal. Acuff tried to test his popularity by quitting the networked Prince Albert portion in 1946, but rather than capitulate to his demands, *The Opry* hired Red Foley away from a rival jamboree. Acuff later returned on *The Opry*'s terms to host the non-networked Royal Crown Cola segment of the show.

In return for almost no pay, *The Opry* offered a loyal audience of millions, assistance in booking shows (for which it took a 15 percent commission), and the indefinable cachet of *Opry* membership. The show's management could make these demands because of its almost biblical importance to its audience. *The Opry* brought country music into isolated hollers and rural homesteads, and to homesick Southerners in big northern cities. It brought families and neighbors together on Saturday night. By the light of coal oil lamps, they'd hook up the radio to the car battery, even if it meant pushing the car on Sunday morning. "We all loved *The Opry*," said Ralph Stanley. "We looked forward to Saturday night, and my father bought this old Philco battery radio in 1936, and it was about the only radio in the area, around where we lived, and a lot of people come in every Saturday night to listen." It was an experience repeated across virtually the breadth of the United States, east of the great plains.

Chapter 8

SONGS FOR
Home Folks

In 1945, as the war ended, Nashville had no professional-quality studios, no session musicians, no record companies, and just one or two music publishers. As late as 1946, Los Angeles, Atlanta, Cincinnati, and above all Chicago were considered the hubs of the country music business. Ten years later, "Nashville" and "country music" were synonymous.

The rise of Nashville went hand in hand with the growing preeminence of *The Grand Ole Opry*. *The Opry* attracted the stars that the country audience wanted to hear. The stars moved to Nashville, and the business followed. It was a disreputable business at first, and the city didn't try to disguise the fact that it was unwelcome. Nashville proclaimed itself "the Athens of the South." The city fathers built a fake Parthenon and wanted Nashville city to become a center of learning, commerce, and government.

Country music didn't fit into this vision at all, and the attitude percolated downward. Car salesmen were told not to sell new automobiles to country music singers because they'd drive them into the ground then default on the payments, leaving the dealership to repossess a worthless vehicle. Musicians found it hard to rent houses or even get a telephone. But country music came anyway. Ernest Tubb, Bill Monroe, Roy Acuff, Red Foley, Pee Wee King, Eddy Arnold, and a host of minor stars were in Nashville every Friday and Saturday night. Song pluggers knew they could pitch songs on those nights; bookers knew they could line up shows; record producers knew they could cut sessions.

above Selling songs to Home Folks: Fred Rose (right) with his son, Wesley.
opposite Hank Williams meetin' and greetin'.

The Nashville music business was almost entirely in the future on October 13, 1942 when Roy Acuff's wife, Mildred, signed a partnership agreement with songwriter Fred Rose to create Nashville's first professional music publishing company, Acuff-Rose Publications. Mildred had been active in publishing Acuff's songbooks, and the Acuffs promised to supply capital if needed, but Rose's reputation was sufficient for Acuff-Rose to receive an advance of $2500 from the BMI. Before long, the company was solvent, but Acuff's name was still important because it attracted writers and performers.

Fred Rose had first come to Nashville in 1933 as a songwriter and radio personality. His songs had been recorded by jazzmen and dance bands for almost a decade. He'd written big jazz age hits such as "Red Hot Mama" and "Deed I Do," as well as topical songs which he often composed "live" on air, but his alcoholism cost him one job after another. In 1935, Rose converted to Christian Science and tried to lick his problem. Endlessly adaptable, he moved to Hollywood and began writing western songs, first for Tex Ritter and then for Gene Autry and other singing cowboys. In 1942, under pressure from his wife, he returned to her hometown, Nashville. Just months later, he formed his partnership with the Acuffs. Rose had written western songs in Hollywood, and now that he was in Nashville he began writing hillbilly and

gospel songs. Acuff was his major customer, and Rose wrote several big hits for his new partner, notably "Blue Eyes Crying in the Rain," which became a number one country hit for Willie Nelson some thirty years after Acuff first recorded it. Rose's major responsibility, though, was to work as a song doctor with the company's writers, then place the songs with artists or A&R men. Live radio was such an important factor that Rose hired a song plugger to go around the South leaving Acuff-Rose sheet music and songbooks at radio stations in the hope that local singers would pick them up and perform the songs.

In January 1943, Rose took out an advertisement in the music industry's trade paper, *Billboard*: "Look out for folk tunes and popular hits from Nashville," he wrote. Three years later, in a letter to *Billboard*, he began extolling his beliefs: "We pride ourselves in being a very intelligent people and good Americans," he wrote, "but are we? We put on our best bib and tucker and make quite an affair of spending an enjoyable evening being entertained with Russian, Italian, French etc. folklore... We read all kinds of books that will give us an understanding of foreign folklore, but what do we say and do about our own good ol' American folklore? We call it 'hillbilly' music and sometimes we're ashamed to call it music... Remember, 75 percent of all the people in the United States like and love simple things and simple music— folklore—and all of them are potential buyers of your music." Rose's conversion to country music was complete, and he now sought to convert others. He appended a little slogan to his company's letterhead, "Songs for Home Folks."

It has never really been explained why Hank Williams boarded a train in Montgomery, Alabama,

above Fred Rose (left) and Roy Acuff.
opposite Nashville during the 1940s.

on September 14, 1946, en route to Acuff-Rose's offices. Fred Rose's son, Wesley, always said that Hank was making a cold call, and Wesley went on to fabricate an elaborate story in which he and Fred were playing ping-pong after lunch when Hank came in unannounced. According to Wesley, Fred listened to Hank, then asked him to go into a side room and write a song on the spot to prove that he had written rather than bought the songs. The result, said Wesley, was "A Mansion on the Hill." In fact, Hank had already published one song via Acuff-Rose. Three years earlier, he had been working with Pee Wee King and sold him a song he'd written, "I'm Praying for the Day (When Peace Will Come)." King brought it back to Nashville and placed it with Acuff-Rose, but Rose couldn't persuade anyone to record it before the end of the

war. By the time Hank arrived in Nashville, Rose was tight with Columbia's A&R man, Art Satherley, and Satherley was scouting songs for a new act he'd signed, Molly O'Day. Molly sang in a style very like Roy Acuff, and she'd not only worked shows in Montgomery with Hank, but acquired songs from him, so she probably told Satherley or Rose to contact Hank for more material. Hank almost certainly arrived in Nashville with songs for Molly O'Day, who would indeed record several of his numbers over the next year or so.

Shortly before Molly O'Day's first session, Rose got a call from Al Middleman, president of a new company, Sterling Records, headquartered in New York. Middleman wanted a hillbilly and gospel line to complement his jazz, pop and R&B series, and he asked Rose to find some hillbilly acts, record them

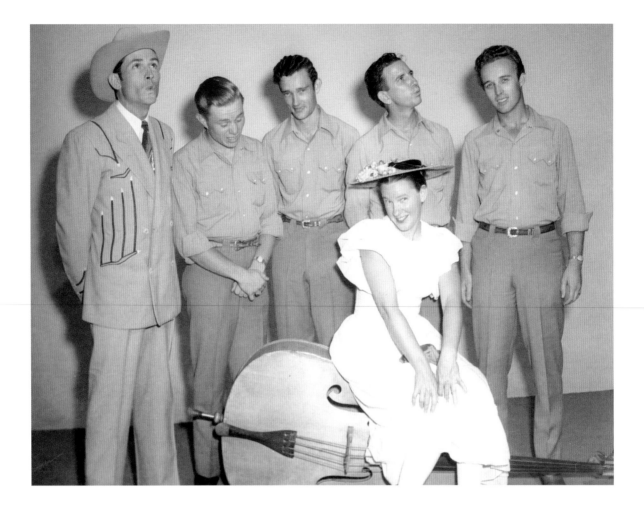

in Nashville, and ship the masters to him. Some say that it was Rose's secretary, Eleanor Shea, who remembered Hank Williams. According to Wesley Rose, he was the one who remembered Hank. According to Hank, Fred Rose's first thought had been to sign another act, Johnnie and Jack, and he was only brought into consideration after they told Rose that they'd just signed with another label. Rose signed a western group at the same time. Three Willis brothers called themselves the Oklahoma Wranglers, and Rose asked them if they would back Hank. They said they would. And so, on the morning of December 11, 1946, Hank Williams recorded his first session.He rehearsed during the morning, then went for lunch at the Clarkston Hotel with the Willises. Everyone was having sandwiches and beer, and the waitress asked Hank if he wanted a beer. "No," Hank replied. "You don't know ol' Hank. Hank don't just have *one* beer." Vic Willis finished before the others and went back to the

studio. Fred Rose asked him if Hank was drinking. Vic said, "No." Rose said, "Good." Just before the session, Rose gave Hank and the Willises a prepared letter in which they agreed to record for union scale ($82.50 for the leader and $41.25 for side men) and waived their rights to future royalties. With his signature, Hank Williams stepped onto the bottom rung of the ladder.

Just over six years later, Hank Williams was dead. In between, he became the most powerfully iconic figure in country music. Iconic to the point that man and myth are inextricably entwined. He set the agenda for contemporary country songcraft and sang his songs with such believability that he seems very real, despite the fact that he left no extended interviews and hugely conflicting memories among those who knew him. The little truths in his songs soon became reduced to clichés, and those clichés were pounced upon by those who disliked country music. Honky-tonkin' and cheatin' hearts. But Hank

Williams' songs were desperately real when he sang them. They were little sonograms of life, certainly *his* life. Beneath them lay the same haunted spirituality that underpinned much of the Stanley Brothers' or Bill Monroe's work. Williams sang of being pursued by the "Pale Horse and His Rider," and when he directly addressed "The Angel of Death," he could bring a chill to any room. He sang as if he'd just seen a video of the rest of his life. It's impossible to escape the feeling that he lived with the spirits every day, and drank in part to escape them.

Hank Williams' star appeared to rise fast, but he'd worked the honky-tonks in south Alabama for ten years by the time he signed with Sterling Records in 1946. The following year, Rose placed him with the newly launched record division of MGM, and his first MGM record, "Move It on Over," became a hit. He was twenty-three then, and twenty-five when his arrangement of "Lovesick Blues," adapted from Rex Griffin's arrangement, became the biggest country hit of 1949.

The Grand Ole Opry had been wary of Hank Williams. Word of his drinking and belligerence had already reached Nashville, but *The Opry* management was worried that Hank would spearhead a rival jamboree, and took a chance on him. Fred Rose sweetened the pot by giving the composer credit on a song he'd written, "Chattanoogie Shoe Shine Boy," to *Opry* manager Harry Stone and WSM manager Jack Stapp. Red Foley later recorded it, and it became the second biggest hit of 1950.

Hank Williams recorded just sixty-six songs under his own name, together with six more as half of a doomed husband-and-wife act, "Hank &

opposite Whistlin' Dixie: Hank Williams (left) with Jerry Rivers, Sammy Pruett, Cedric Rainwater, Don Helms, and Minnie Pearl.
right Hank Williams and the Drifting Cowboys on stage.

Audrey," and another fourteen released under his moralistic *alter ego*, "Luke the Drifter." Of the sixty-six regular session recordings, an astonishing thirty-seven were hits. More than once, he cut three songs that became standards in one afternoon. The fourteen Luke the Drifter recordings were mostly narrations. Luke the Drifter walked with Hank Williams and talked through him. If Hank Williams could be a backslider and a reprobate, then Luke

the Drifter was compassionate and moralistic, able to dispense all the sage advice that Hank Williams ignored. Luke the Drifter had seen it all, yet could still be moved to tears by a chance encounter on his travels. Unlike the recordings that Williams issued under his own name, some of the Luke the Drifter recordings have become woefully dated.

Fred Rose returned to his background in topical songs to write the Red-baiting "No, No, Joe" (aimed at Josef Stalin). "The Colored Child's Funeral" was a popular poem in the early 1900s, and Hank recited it, clearly extending every ounce of compassion within him, but it too was a piece that doesn't wear

its age well. Hank also released a few talking blues as Luke the Drifter. One of them, "Please Make up Your Mind," ranks among the most rivetingly vengeful songs ever written. If comedy is the public face of private darkness, then his marriage to Audrey had been a desperately unhappy one. He'd pitched the song to fellow Opry star Little Jimmy Dickens in 1951, but when he recorded it himself a year later, he omitted one couplet from the Dickens version: "The preacher man said, 'For better or worse,'/But lately I been looking for that big black

hearse." Hank Williams had twenty-five weeks to live on the day he recorded it.

As a songwriter, Hank Williams matured surprisingly quickly, and his fractious relationship with Audrey provided him with most of the raw material. Fred Rose guided him, goaded him, and taught him commercial songcraft. In letters that Hank kept, Rose berated him for his drinking binges, offering detailed advice on relationships and music. Hank wrote compulsively, and Rose would sift through the song fragments that Hank brought

left Hank Williams (seated center) with promoter Dub Allbritten (standing) in Texas, 1952.

1951, and from that point there was a rush to reinterpret every one of his songs for the pop market. Ironically, those pop versions, which comfortably outsold the originals in the early 1950s, now sound over-ornamented and outdated, while the spare and haunting originals do not.

Contrary to myth, Hank Williams did not die with his star in the ascendant. His last major hit, "Jambalaya," was one of the best-selling records of 1952, but he was so unreliable that he was reduced to playing beerhalls in Texas. *The Opry* dismissed him in August 1952, then tried to reclaim him in death. *The Opry* management insisted that he would have returned to the show in February 1953 had he not died on January 1, but surviving correspondence suggests nothing more than a few more beerhall gigs in Hank Williams' future.

Timing is everything, and Hank Williams came and went at precisely the right time. Country music was a cottage industry when he began his career in south Alabama, but the war sent country boys far and wide. Some went into the service, some went up North to the munitions plants, others went out west to the shipyards. Country music went everywhere they went. Hank Williams toured California and Canada, worked a short stint in Las Vegas, and was on his way to northern Ohio when he died. He probably wouldn't have toured as far afield if he'd arrived a decade earlier.

In December 1954, almost two years after Williams died, Fred Rose suffered a heart attack in the studio and died shortly afterward. His Christian Science beliefs had enabled him to kick his drinking habit, but prevented him from seeking the medical attention that might have saved him.

back from his road trips, isolating those that held promise. The very best of the songs that Hank Williams wrote under Fred Rose's tutelage rank among the finest country songs of all time. "You Win Again," "Your Cheatin' Heart," "I Can't Help It (If I'm Still in Love with You)," "I'm So Lonesome I Could Cry," and "Cold, Cold Heart" are taut and concise. Not a word or inflection is wasted. They relate everyday concerns in words that still seem fresh. Williams' songs began to find a wider market after Tony Bennett covered "Cold, Cold Heart" in

Chapter 9

You Might HAVE SOMETHING *with This Hillbilly Thing...*

In the Summer of 1950, Dick Stratton and the Nite Owls recorded a song called "Music City USA." It had a sing-song melody and a tag-line that went, "They used to call it Nashville but I'm here to say/ That now they call it Music City USA." Goofy as it was, it proved that in just a few years Nashville really had become the hub of the country music business.

With the rise of Nashville, there was a country mainstream for the first time. In 1945, country music was many, very separate things: old-time fiddling and square dance music, stringbands, western swing, cowboy music, honky-tonk, smooth country-pop, hillbilly music, bluegrass, brother duets, and sacred quartets. Ten years later, the industry had settled in Nashville and there was a mainstream sound. Newer artists, such as Webb Pierce, Faron Young, Carl Smith, or Marty Robbins, used much the same instrumentation, and often the same musicians and songwriters. Older forms of country music became marginalized. New artists had to fit into the mainstream or the record companies would be reluctant to sign them.

The country record business was in remarkably few hands: just a handful of men, most of them headquartered a long way from Nashville, and none of them from the South. The major labels had dominated country music from the beginning and never surrendered control. Independent record labels, such as Chess, Atlantic, and Imperial, ruled postwar R&B, but no independent label gained more than a toehold in country music. The independents seemed unable to do more than record styles deemed unsalesworthy by the majors.

above Owen Bradley.
opposite Lefty Frizzell and his Cadillac.

Fred Rose and Roy Acuff started Hickory Records in 1954, and it became Nashville's most long-lived independent label, but it wasn't the first. Some nine years earlier, a small consortium of entrepreneurs and flimflam men started Bullet Records. If the Bullet partners had played their cards right, their label might have rivaled the majors. "It was 1945," said former *Opry* booking agent Jim Bulleit. "I was walking down Broad Street with a gospel singer named Wally Fowler. Out of the blue he turned and said, 'Jim, how would you like to go into the record business?' He took me into a store on Broad called Hermitage Music to meet a man named C. V. Hitchcock. He said, 'Mister Hitchcock thinks we can make a go of recording.' We talked for about fifteen minutes and when I got out of the store I was in the record business. Nashville in 1945 was really not geared up to the music business at all. There was *The Opry*, but I was practically the only booking agent in town. The only studios were owned by the radio stations, and the only music publisher in town was Fred Rose. It seems obvious now, but the logical step was to form a record company dealing in the country music that was promoted by *The Opry*."

The partners' big idea was that they would sign every unsigned *Opry* act and ride on *The Opry*'s coat-tails. It was a sweet deal for C.V. Hitchcock, who owned a jukebox business and liked the cost-efficiency of putting his own records on his machines. For his part, Bulleit seemed drawn to any wildly entrepreneurial scheme. The first release on Bullet was by "Brad Brady," who turned out to be Owen Bradley. At the time, Bradley was leading a pop orchestra on WSM, and, like the rest of Nashville, didn't want to be associated with the hillbillies. "Our 1000 sales estimate escalated to 9000," Bulleit said later, "and Owen came to me and said, 'Jim, I think you might have something with this hillbilly thing. If it would be alright with you, I just might like to put my real name on the record after all.'" Bullet went on to release the first records by several country legends, including Ray Price, Chet Atkins, Minnie Pearl, and Pee Wee King. Bullet also released B. B. King's first records, and scored one of the biggest pop hits of all time with Francis Craig's "Near You." Craig led a pop orchestra on WSM, and chart statistics confirm that no record ever spent longer at number one than "Near You." Bullet used some of the money to start the first pressing plant in Nashville, but by 1952 the label was bankrupt. The partners developed grandiose visions and signed pop acts, such as Bing Crosby's brother. The pop sessions cost thousands, whereas hillbilly and R&B sessions usually cost no more than $300 or $400. If the partners had stayed with what they knew, Bullet might have remained successful.

Bullet found what every independent label found: it is almost impossible to crack the major labels' hammerlock on country music. Hickory Records was in business for just over thirty years, but became a retirement home for Acuff-Rose artists/songwriters who could no longer get better deals (and, as of 1957, this included Acuff himself). Other independent labels came and went. Some looked like contenders, but the majors were always in the wings with their checkbooks waiting to poach any minor label artist who looked likely to amount to anything. Bullet lost Owen Bradley, Chet Atkins, Ray Price, and Pee Wee King to the majors.

In 1945, there were three major labels, RCA, Columbia, and Decca, all headquartered in New York. Capitol Records had been launched in Los Angeles in 1942, but had become so successful so quickly that it

almost ranked as a major label by the end of the war. RCA bundled country music with blues, gospel, comedy, and kids' music into its Specialty Singles Division. Steve Sholes headed the department, but remained in New York. His division was profitable, but derided within the company. "In sales meetings, when it got to Steve's department, a lot of guys would say, 'Hey, I gotta go to the john,'" recalled field rep, Brad McCuen. Sholes himself remembered the same thing. "I was never allowed to play more than six or eight revolutions of one of my records," he said. "The gospel records I wasn't permitted to play at all: just announce the titles. There was no attention paid to merchandising, special merchandising, or *any* merchandising. There was no promotion or publicity to speak of."

Sholes' background was in classical music, but he developed a true love of country music. He went to shows when he was in the South, and listened compulsively. Even when he took his family to the beach, he'd bring a little portable record player to check out new songs. Going to shows, Sholes realized that the country music audience was old.

opposite Don Law.
above Paul Cohen (second right) with Patsy Cline.

below Eddy Arnold at home with his wife, Sally.
inset Ken Nelson (center) with the Louvin Brothers.

The kids weren't coming. Sholes knew he had to rectify that problem, and eventually he would.

From 1929 until 1967, Columbia Records' country music division was the preserve of two Englishmen, Art Satherley and his assistant, Don Law. Despite his background, Satherley truly understood the music. "Sing it in the extreme," he would tell the vocalists. "We don't care about trick ways of phrasing or hot licks; we concentrate on the emotions." Satherley and Law worked together throughout most of the 1930s and '40s, but in 1951 Columbia divided responsibility for its country division between them. Law signed two big stars, Lefty Frizzell and Carl Smith, while Satherley's signings did comparatively little business at the time, although Marty Robbins became one of the label's mainstays. And so, in May 1952, Satherley was dismissed, despite the fact that his past signees included Bob Wills, Gene Autry, Roy Acuff, and Bill Monroe. Satherley found to his cost that the record business credo is, "What have you done for me lately?" Law had spent some years in Dallas and preferred to record there, but slowly bowed to the inevitable and began scheduling Nashville sessions. Like Sholes, he remained in New York, and commuted to Nashville several times a year.

Decca's country A&R chief was Chicago-born Paul Cohen, who had been with the company since it began as an offshoot of British Decca in 1934. Cohen took over responsibility for country music in 1944, and signed Webb Pierce, Kitty Wells, Brenda Lee, and Patsy Cline. RCA held the first modern recording session in Nashville when it recorded Eddy Arnold at the WSM studio in December 1944, but Cohen was the first to realize the benefits of scheduling regular sessions in Nashville. On August 30, 1947, *Billboard* reported, "Red Foley cut [his] first Decca platters in Nashville two weeks ago.

Previously all cutting was done in Chicago." Cohen soon began relying heavily on Owen Bradley (now fully converted to "this hillbilly thing") as his field rep while he remained in New York.

Of all the majors, Capitol Records was the one with the least commitment to Nashville. From 1951 until 1976, the label's country music chief was a dry, ascetic Northerner named Ken Nelson. When journalist John Grissim interviewed him in the mid-1960s, he described him as looking like an amiable Midwestern dry goods dealer. "He lives outside fashion," wrote Grissim, "the consummate practitioner of his craft." Nelson flew to Nashville several times a year to record his few locally based artists, but didn't have a permanent Nashville office until the 1960s. Unlike Law and Cohen, Ken Nelson didn't go drinking with his artists, and, alone among the major label A&R men, didn't buy into the notion of Nashville as "Music City USA." For RCA, Columbia, and Decca, though, "Nashville" and "country music" were synonymous by 1950.

Every label had hugely successful mainstays. RCA's Eddy Arnold was highly popular and sold millions of records before, during, and after Hank Williams. In terms of sales, Williams never came close to eclipsing him. In 1947, Arnold sold an unprecedented 2.7 million records, and was so successful the following year that just one other artist managed to get a record to number one. For all but six weeks of 1948, Eddy Arnold was at the top of the charts, and his hit streak continued through the early 1950s and beyond. Unlike Hank Williams, Arnold's music holds no dark covenants, and betrays no insecurity or pain. He came from rural poverty in west Tennessee, but his well-disguised ambition led him to make some good gambles, and his genuine bonhomie seemed to win over audiences. He was a natural, unabashed

right Flying the flag for country music in Germany, 1949. From left: Rod Brasfield, unknown serviceman, Red Foley, Jimmy Dickens, Minnie Pearl, Hank Williams, unknown service personnel.

populist who oversaw country music's evolution from folk to pop-based material, and played a major role in that transition. More than anyone, Eddy Arnold brought country music to a wider audience. His songs weren't covered by the pop crooners because he was already more than halfway toward pop, but whereas Hank Williams' songs are still sung and recorded today, many of Arnold's songs were period pieces that haven't weathered the years too well. In many ways, Arnold's success was a dry run for Elvis Presley, and this might have been no accident because both careers were orchestrated by the same man, Colonel Tom Parker. Between 1943 and 1953, Parker managed Eddy Arnold, pulling the same carny stunts that he would later employ on behalf of Elvis, and with much the same results. Parker took a country singer and brought him to a nationwide audience. He didn't try to influence the music; in fact, probably didn't even think about the music. He just saw Arnold, watched the audience, and began projecting. It was all about sales.

Decca's Red Foley followed in Arnold's wake, but is largely forgotten today. Pat Boone eloped with his daughter and Elvis immortalized his dying dog song, "Old Shep," but Foley's smooth, unruffled vocal style became an artistic dead end. Lefty Frizzell sold millions fewer records than Eddy Arnold or Red Foley, but had an immeasurably greater influence. He brought the sound of the east Texas honky-tonks into the Nashville era. Merle Haggard once said, "Lefty Frizzell was the most unique thing that ever happened to country music," and from Haggard's perspective, he was. Frizzell began as a Jimmie Rodgers disciple in the Texas, Arkansas, and

Louisiana oilfields, but developed a vocal style that suggested more vulnerability than anyone had ever suggested to that point. He bent notes, lingered over vowels, twisted and deconstructed phrases. It was a style for which the microphone was a prerequisite. Young singers were in awe of Lefty Frizzell. "The first singer I heard on the radio who really slayed me was Lefty Frizzell," said Roy Orbison, who grew up in west Texas. "He had this technique which involved sliding syllables together that really blew me away." Roy and his father, Orbie, went to see Lefty. They pulled into the parking lot and saw a car sticking out ten feet further than all other cars. It was Lefty's Cadillac,

and the image seared itself into Roy Orbison's brain. You could drive out of west Texas in that Cadillac. When Orbison signed a buddy's high school yearbook it was as "Roy 'Lefty Frizzell' Orbison," and when he joined the Traveling Wilburys toward the end of his life it was as Lefty Wilbury.

Lefty was always in trouble. He was arrested for statutory rape in 1947, and signed so many contracts that, at the peak of his success, he was giving away 115 percent of what he earned. He drank heavily throughout his life and was chronically unreliable, but he wrested several songs of enduring beauty from the catastrophe of his life. "I Love You a Thousand Ways" (a valentine to his

wife written from jail), "Always Late," and "Mom and Dad's Waltz" were heartwrenchingly tender songs, especially when Frizzell enveloped them in his unique style. He also wrote one of the great, postwar honky-tonk anthems, "If You've Got the Money, I've Got the Time." Don Law signed him to Columbia in June 1950, and Lefty's star rose meteorically but fell just as fast. And unlike Hank Williams, he lived long enough to make some very mediocre records.

Decca Records' mainstay throughout the early 1950s was Webb Pierce. Singing high and frequently off-key, Pierce came from north Louisiana but went to Nashville as quickly as he could. His records had an identifiably Nashville sound: taut, economical, and nasal. Pierce had three gifts: natural flamboyance, excellent business sense, and an almost infallible ear for a great song. To his discredit, he not only insisted on publishing many of those great songs but also insisted on cutting himself in for half of the composer credit whenever possible. He thus got the publisher's 50 percent share, and half of the writer's 50 percent share. Many young songwriters got an early break writing for Webb Pierce, but that break came at a cost. Pierce, though, wouldn't let publishing stand in the way of recording a song he really believed in, and several of his hits addressed serious issues with brutal frankness.

Both Fred Rose and *Opry* manager Jim Denny told Pierce that "There Stands the Glass" would derail his career. Rose collared Pierce backstage at *The Opry*. "This time you've forever done it," he told him. "It doesn't even have a moral. It tolerates drinking." Pierce, though, knew better. "You're singing about something that 80 percent of people do," he said later. "They say, 'Heck, that ole record over there is my friend. I'll go play it again.'" Many radio stations wouldn't touch it, but it spent twelve weeks atop the charts in 1953. Pierce knew that the song's power came from the fact that it didn't moralize. It said, "Hell, yes, I'm drinking."

Pierce also challenged 1950s' morality in "Back Street Affair," which was written from personal experience by an Alabama singer-songwriter named Billy Wallace. Pierce heard Hank Williams sing it on the radio and assumed that it was Williams' new record. "Naw, it ain't my new record," Williams told him. "Fred Rose won't let me record it. Too risky. I think anyone's got guts enough to record it has got themselves a number one hit." Within days, Pierce was in the studio, and Williams lived just long enough to see his prophecy fulfilled. Twenty-five straight hits ensured that Webb Pierce was country music's biggest star in the years after Williams' death. In later life, he became a cartoon character, encrusting a Pontiac with silver dollars and building a guitar-shaped swimming pool. When tourists came to gawp, he'd pose for photos and direct them toward a rack of records for sale. His business acumen not only led him to start a music publishing company, Cedarwood Music, that became one of country music's great catalogs, but also led him to realize the increasing power of the disc-jockey. The live radio era was disappearing and several 50,000-watt powerhouse stations featured night-time dee-jay shows that blanketed most of the country. Pierce not only recognized this trend but courted the disc-jockeys, and, by some accounts, introduced payola to the country record business.

Hank Snow's strange, maverick career was a monument to dogged persistence. On October 10, 1936, he recorded his first session for RCA Victor in a dark, cold, abandoned church in Montreal, Canada. On November 19, 1980, he wrapped up his last session for the label in Nashville. Born in Dickensian poverty in the Canadian Maritimes, abused and humiliated as a child, Snow worked desperately hard to achieve stardom. Until Shania Twain, he was Canada's only country superstar. He wanted to be on RCA because his idol, Jimmie Rodgers, had been on the label, and he stayed truer to the spirit of Rodgers' music than other disciples, such as Gene Autry, Ernest Tubb, or Lefty Frizzell. Realizing that he must break out of the small Canadian market, Snow tried repeatedly to interest the American parent company in his songs, but it wasn't until March 1949 that he recorded his first session outside Canada. On his third American

opposite Webb Pierce.

session, he persuaded Steve Sholes to let him record a song he'd written, "I'm Moving On." On August 19, 1950, it reached number one and stayed there for twenty-one weeks. No song ever stayed longer. Snow wrote many of his biggest hits and played his own acoustic lead guitar. The bright, ringing sound of his solos was just one of the factors that made his records unique.

Many of Hank Snow's faster songs had the giddiness and goofiness of rockabilly. Songs such as "Rhumba Boogie" ("While Madame Mazonga was teaching the conga in a little cabana in old Havana") had a generation of future rockabillies sitting up nights picking them apart. After Colonel Parker severed his relationship with Eddy Arnold, he formed a partnership with Hank Snow, and their

company, Jamboree Attractions, booked Snow and several younger artists, including Elvis Presley. Snow played a decisive role in bringing Elvis to RCA, but when the smoke cleared, he insisted that he had been shuffled out of the deal. His loyalty to RCA was no better rewarded: he audited the company, only to discover that he had been cheated out of half a million dollars in royalties. RCA then

terminated his contract in 1981, five years shy of the fifty years that Snow desperately wanted to achieve. Bitterness became the prevailing motif of his last years.

Just two years and two months separated Hank Williams' last appearance on *The Grand Ole Opry* from Elvis Presley's sole *Opry* appearance. When musicologists write about the birth of rock 'n' roll it's usually in terms of white kids going for the passion and the rhythms of R&B, but there was much more to it than that. The goofiness of rockabilly owed much to Hank Snow. Rock 'n' roll attitude owed much to Webb Pierce's flamboyance. The Everly Brothers drew on the sound of the country brother duets. Roy Orbison wanted to be Lefty Frizzell. The fierce confrontationalism of bluegrass gave rockabilly its fire. "If you'd put an electric guitar and a set of drums behind Bill Monroe in 1938, you'd have had rockabilly music fifteen years earlier," says Dwight Yoakam. "Put on Bill Monroe singing 'Rocky Road Blues' and I'll show you where rock 'n' roll got 50 percent of its cool." Monroe's "Blue Moon of Kentucky" entered rock 'n' roll via Elvis Presley; and "Rocky Road Blues" became a hit for Gene Vincent.

RCA's Steve Sholes wrote an article for *Cashbox* magazine in 1954 in which he talked about the necessity of drawing a younger audience to country music. Later that year, he and Colonel Parker devised a country caravan show designed to bring country music out of the honky-tonks and into auditoriums where kids could hear it. And then, in 1955, the Colonel told Sholes that he had a young country artist who was driving the kids crazy. Sholes, of course, was all ears.

left Hank Snow attends to business at the Rainbow Ranch.

Chapter 10

THE KING
of Western Bop

On August 28, 1954, Elvis Presley's version of Bill Monroe's "Blue Moon of Kentucky" entered *Billboard*'s Memphis country chart on the tiny Sun label. No one, of course, could have foreseen the ramifications of that little entry. Elvis was a listener—a voracious listener. We know he listened to R&B and black gospel music, but he listened just as voraciously to country music.

Elvis's familiarity with country shouldn't astonish anyone. He came from Mississippi's white underclass. Country music was the soundtrack to the Presleys' life. Its mantras would have been desperately familiar to them: hard times, jail, dying mothers, Saturday night Satans and Sunday saints. *The Grand Ole Opry* on Saturday night was as much a part of Elvis's young life as Gene Autry shoot 'em ups on Saturday morning.

Elvis talked about seeing blues singer Arthur "Big Boy" Crudup in Tupelo, Mississippi, and it's a compelling image: the skinny, awestruck pre-teen watching the towering blues singer "bang his box," as Elvis memorably put it. But Elvis could just as easily have talked about going to see Mississippi Slim at radio station WELO in Tupelo. Slim hosted a show called *Pickin' and Singin' Hillbilly*, and for a while in 1945 and 1946, Slim epitomized all the glamor of the music business for ten- or eleven-year-old Elvis Presley. The customized guitar, the fringed suit, the easy patter. It was everything Elvis wanted. When he first sang in public in 1945, it wasn't an Arthur Crudup song, but Red Foley's "Old Shep." The blues was a private passion. Elvis gave no thought to

above Steve Sholes welcomes Elvis to RCA.
opposite Elvis on the *Louisiana Hayride*.

singing the blues until Sun Records owner Sam Phillips caught him goofing off on Crudup's "That's All Right." The song Elvis was trying to cut that night was a 1940s' country hit, "I Love You Because." It survived on tape as a little reminder of what was on Elvis's mind five minutes before he invented rockabilly. When Sam Phillips took delivery of the first pressing of "That's All Right"/"Blue Moon of Kentucky," he knew he had something unique, but was probably unsure what to do with it. Was it pop, R&B, or country? Where would Elvis perform? Phillips had worked for years in mainstream pop radio and had engineered big band broadcasts from the Hotel Peabody in Memphis, so he knew that Elvis and his little two-piece band didn't belong in that world. Elvis's sound was too spare and too country for R&B. The only option was to take him to country radio and to get him on some country shows.

Elvis's first chart appearances were on local country charts; his first national chart entry ("I'm Left, You're Right, She's Gone") was in the country charts; his first shows were at country nightspots; his first major appearance was on a Slim Whitman show; his first radio broadcasts were on Saturday night radio barn dances, such as *The Opry*, *Louisiana Hayride*, and *Big "D" Jamboree*; and his first tours were with country package shows. From the beginning, Elvis was "alternative country," not as a conscious anti-Nashville aesthetic, but because that's what he was. He had grown up listening to *The Grand Ole Opry*, and some part of him probably wanted to play The *Opry* every week, but his one *Opry* appearance confirmed that he didn't belong there. Instead, Elvis made Sun Records and, in a

broader sense, Memphis, into a magnet for those who couldn't or wouldn't play the Nashville game. Carl Perkins' tapes had been returned by every label in Nashville. Jerry Lee Lewis had left Nashville unsigned and unheard before coming to Sun. Johnny Cash knew better than even to try to interest anyone in Nashville in what he was doing. They all ended up on Sun Records in Elvis's wake.

By late 1955, every country A&R chief with the possible exception of Don Law had contacted Sam Phillips about buying Elvis's contract, but Phillips' price was always ahead of what they were willing to pay, and by the time they were willing to meet the price, it had gone up. Meanwhile, Colonel Parker finagled his way onto Elvis's management team. He brought his partner, Hank Snow, to Memphis to impress Mr. and Mrs. Presley, and began his campaign to get Elvis off Sun. He talked to Steve Sholes, and arranged to showcase Elvis to Sholes during the Nashville dee-jays convention on November 10, 1955. Phillips' price was now $35,000 plus $5000 in unpaid back royalties. It was an unprecedented amount for a country singer with almost no hits, but Sholes agreed. Sam Phillips had guaranteed to hold the price firm until November 15, and Parker wired Phillips that day to tell him that the deal was done. Anxious not to lose this opportunity of getting Elvis off Sun, Parker fronted his own money to purchase the option before Phillips' deadline.

"A great many people in and out of RCA figured that Steve Sholes had just aced himself out of the business," said RCA field rep Brad McCuen. Elvis's first RCA session was an epic cultural collision. He left Memphis on January 10, 1956, and arrived at RCA's Nashville studio shortly before 2:00 PM. RCA, like all major labels, expected its country artists to record four songs in three hours with local union

musicians. Elvis worked from 2:00 PM until 10:00 PM, then clocked up another three-hour session the following day. He used his own band as the nucleus of the group, and emerged with just five songs. That was the way he'd worked at Sun, and it says much about his strange solipsism that he never even thought of accommodating RCA. Chet Atkins was there, and later told one of the Jordanaires, Gordon Stoker, that Elvis was just another flash in the pan.

From the beginning, Sholes saw Elvis's crossover potential. He pressured sales manager John Burgess, who in turn pressured his staff. Sholes knew that his career was on the line. "It's imperative that you follow up this all-market approach to every station receiving Pop or Country

service," Burgess wrote to his reps. "Use the trade articles to sell your dealers and one-stops *across the board*." Sholes was now consumed with everything Presley. "Steve used to fly down to Nashville and do maybe three days of sessions," said Brad McCuen, "but then the Colonel would want to see him in Chicago or somewhere, and Steve would call up Chet and say, 'Hey, I can't make it. Can you do it?' And Chet would say, 'Why, certainly.'"

Within months of signing to RCA, Elvis triggered a three-alarm panic attack in Nashville. Country dee-jays, a relatively new species, began chasing the youth dollar. They spun Elvis's records and rockabilly records, squeezing out the older artists. Booking agent Hal Smith handled Ernest Tubb at

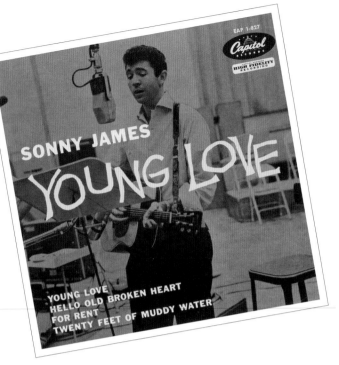

the time. "We came to the conclusion that the best thing to do would be to get out of the business," Smith told researcher Ronnie Pugh. "Ernest's brother was in the insurance business in Texas, so he said, 'I could go into business with Bud, but this is all I've ever done.' It was so sad." Tubb in fact hung in there long enough to see his career revive, but things looked bleak in 1956. Television was tempting country music's traditional crowd to stay at home, and, as Steve Sholes had seen, the teenagers didn't want older country music. Even *The Grand Ole Opry* was three-quarters empty some nights, and NBC dropped it from the network schedule in 1957. It was one of those moments, like the end of the Second World War or the onset of the Great Depression, when all bets were off, and no one knew what would happen next.

Elvis had been signed by RCA's country division, so the head offices brought pressure on Paul Cohen, Don Law, and Ken Nelson to find the "next Elvis." Hundreds of young hopefuls were sucked in and spat out. A few, such as Buddy Holly, Johnny Burnette, and Conway Twitty, would resurface another place another time, but most were cut loose after one or two sessions. Older artists tried changing their styles. Webb Pierce recorded a vocal version of Bill Justis's hit instrumental "Raunchy" and tried covering the Everly Brothers' "Bye, Bye Love;" Ernest Tubb recorded Chuck Berry's "Maybellene;" and Marty Robbins recorded an album, *Rockin' Rollin' Robbins*. It wasn't the answer. Looking back on that era, Faron Young concluded, "Hell, we all started trying to put a bit of that jiggery in there. You're making a quarter million a year, and suddenly you're down to $75–$80,000, you'll do anything."

Slowly, it became clear that Elvis represented an opportunity more than a threat, because he'd opened up pop radio. Pop singers had been singing country songs from the beginning ("Prisoner's Song," "You Are My Sunshine," "Pistol Packin' Mama," etc.), but the trend heated up in the late 1940s. Virtually every major country hit was "covered" for the pop market. "Jealous Heart," "Tennessee Waltz," "Slippin' Around," and most of Hank Williams' biggest songs became pop hits for artists such as Patti Page, Tony Bennett, Frankie Laine, and Guy Mitchell. The same thing happened with R&B songs: "Wheel of Fortune," "Hearts of Stone," "Sincerely," and others became giant pop hits. After Elvis, country and R&B songs could reach across the great divide and get on mainstream pop radio if they were not too country or too black.

Capitol's Ken Nelson either saw the possibility or lucked into it. He had two struggling artists on his roster, Ferlin Husky and Sonny James. Husky worked Bakersfield beerjoints and James played Southern barn dances, and they'd both recorded for Capitol since 1952. Husky had seen a few hits; James had seen none. At the end of October 1956, Ken Nelson flew to Nashville. An Atlanta music publisher named Bill Lowery had given him a record by a kid named Ric Cartey. Lowery wanted to license the record to a major label. The top side was a rockabilly tune, "Ooh-Eee," and the flip side was a song that Cartey and his girlfriend had composed, "Young Love."

Steve Sholes licensed the disc, but Nelson told Lowery that he would like Sonny James to do the song on the B-side, and Lowery agreed. It wasn't a song about drinking, cheating, dying mothers, or train wrecks; it was about young love. Nelson sensed that it needed a new backdrop. Out went the fiddle, the banjo, and the steel guitar; in came the electric guitar and a chorus. James was from rural Alabama, but sounded curiously placeless. The regionality and nasality had gone, along with the hard country instruments. The result was easily digestible by pop radio. One week later, Nelson was still in town and Ferlin Husky came in. Four years earlier, Husky had recorded a ballad called "Gone." He now re-recorded it, but the country instruments had been replaced and the chorus was up in the mix. By February 1957, "Young Love" was at number one on the pop charts, and "Gone" was right behind it.

The situation was now clearer to the Nashville A&R men and music publishers: there was no point in older country singers doing rock 'n' roll; the challenge was to find singers who could sing convincingly about "Young Love." Marty Robbins thought he could go where Sonny James had gone. Back in 1955, he'd had covered Elvis's first record, "That's All Right," and he, not Elvis, had scored the hit. Robbins followed it with a rock 'n' roll album that he hated with all his heart. By late 1955, he'd decided to stand or fall with a straight country song, "Singing the Blues," and it surprised everyone by becoming one of the biggest country songs of 1956. It was covered for the pop market by Guy Mitchell, and Robbins was outraged because Mitchell was on his label, Columbia Records. Robbins knew that his record had sold

around 750,000 copies while Mitchell's had sold 3 million. He felt that Mitchell's chance should have been his, and insisted on recording in New York with Mitchell's producer, Mitch Miller, and arranger Ray Conniff. In January 1957, Marty Robbins went to New York with four songs very much like "Young Love." One of them, "A White Sport Coat and a Pink Carnation," became a number two pop hit. For the next eighteen months, Robbins recorded in New York before deciding once again that he would stand or fall with country music.

Sonny James, Ferlin Husky, and Marty Robbins had shown the way, but the record that really sent country music in a new direction was Jim Reeves' "Four Walls." Unlike "Young Love" and "White Sport Coat," it was a country song.

Jim Reeves' career had taken off at the *Louisiana Hayride* barn dance in Shreveport. His first hit came

with a borderline racist novelty song, "Mexican Joe." Elvis joined the *Hayride* a year later, so Reeves had a front-row seat for the birth of rockabilly, but wanted no part of it. Steve Sholes bought his contract from the tiny Abbott label in 1955, and Reeves moved to Nashville. Chet Atkins took over Reeves' sessions after Sholes became consumed with all things Presley. Atkins took his cue from "Young Love" and "A White Sport Coat." Out went the fiddle and steel guitar, and in came the piano, electric guitar, vibraphone, strings, and vocal chorus. "Four Walls" was the first great "Nashville Sound" record. Its quiet, claustrophobic desperation ushered in the new era: "Four walls to hear me, four walls to see/Four walls too near me, closing in on me." The demo and lead-sheet were sitting in a pile on Atkins' desk that toppled over into the trash. Reeves retrieved them, read through the lyrics, and told Atkins he'd like to cut it. "It was a lot of stress," Atkins told journalist Dave Bussey, "because I had to run back and forth to the control room, but Jim liked my guitar sound and wanted me to play the introduction and the bridge. He also wanted the Jordanaires, and I called and couldn't get them. Jim said he wanted that sound, so we moved the session back to when we could get them. He also wanted to rehearse the song, and we were both working on WSM, and we arranged to rehearse 'Four Walls' one evening after the radio program. The Jordanaires were there too. All great things are an accident. You don't just sit down and say, 'I'm going to develop this or that.' I wasn't trying to change the business, just sell records. I realized at that time you had to surprise the public

and give them something a little different. At that time, we had an engineer from New York who was from the old school and he didn't believe in artists getting too close to the microphone in case they popped a 'p' into it. Jim wanted an intimate sound and wanted to get real close and whisper the lyrics, and he had many arguments with this engineer. Then it so happened that we recorded 'Four Walls' with [engineer] Selby Coffeen. Steve Sholes was amazed. He said, 'How did you get that beautiful vocal sound?'" Reeves sang in a warm, enveloping baritone with no trace of his dirt-poor east Texas background. "Four Walls" was almost embarrassingly intimate. It reached number eleven on the pop charts and topped the country charts. Much of what happened in Nashville over the next ten years was predicated by that record. Country producers would evermore have one eye on the pop charts.

opposite Marty Robbins: "A White Sport Coat and a Pink Carnation."
above Jim Reeves in the RCA studio, with Chet Atkins behind the glass.

Chapter 11

BAKERSFIELD, *California*

By the end of the 1950s, "the Nashville Sound" was a phrase on everyone's lips. It first appeared in a Nashville trade paper, *Music Reporter*, in 1958, and *Time* magazine picked up on it in 1960. It almost seemed to create a self-fulfilling prophecy in that records from Nashville quickly developed a uniformity.

The consistent sound stemmed in part from the relatively small pool of session musicians and songwriters, and from the fact that RCA's Chet Atkins, Decca's Owen Bradley, and Columbia's Don Law produced most of the sessions, but it also stemmed from a desire to ape whatever was successful. Jim Reeves was followed by Don Gibson (his original versions of "Oh Lonesome Me" and "I Can't Stop Loving You" were released on the same single in early 1958), Bobby Helms ("Fraulein," "My Special Angel"), the Browns ("The Three Bells," "Scarlet Ribbons"), and Hank Locklin ("Send Me the Pillow You Dream On" and "Please Help Me, I'm Falling").

Every one of those early Nashville Sound records found a level of pop airplay that would have been unthinkable a decade earlier. In November 1960, *Time* magazine revealed that Nashville had edged out Hollywood as the nation's second-largest recording center, and that one in five of the year's top pop hits had been recorded there (although that figure was skewed by the fact that Elvis, Roy Orbison, and the Everlys recorded in Nashville). In 1945, Acuff-Rose was the only music publisher in Nashville; by 1960, there were more than 100. There were 1000 members of the Nashville local of the musicians' union,

above Buck Owens.
opposite Tommy Collins in the Capitol studio with Buck Owens (seated with guitar) and fiddle player Jelly Sanders.

Harold Hensley Speedy West Eddie Kirk Tennessee Ernie Buddy Cobbs Billy Liebert Herman the Hermit

**CLIFFIE STONE'S
HOME TOWN JAMBOREE**

and so many booking agents that, according to the *Time* article, "they have to wear badges to keep from booking each other."

Out in California, the Bakersfield Sound stood in stark contrast to that of Nashville. Bakersfield and Nashville were parallel universes. Bakersfield was the music that Nashville forgot. Warped and hardened in the isolation of the California honky-tonks, it was steel guitars and Fender Telecasters playing off each other. Drums made it danceable. It was music that had migrated from Oklahoma, Texas, and Arkansas, kept alive as a statement about roots in the vast melting pot of Southern California. It was called the Bakersfield Sound, but it could be heard in pockets all around greater Los Angeles. There was a little bit of rock 'n' roll in the Bakersfield Sound, notably in the pinched, stinging tone of the Fender Telecasters, and there was a hint of western swing too, but it was more a natural progression from 1940s' honky-tonk music. It was fiddle, steel guitar, Telecaster, drums, and piercing harmonies on the chorus, and although it could be heard all across greater Los

Angeles and out into the San Joaquin Valley, it began in Bakersfield beerjoints such as the Blackboard Café, Bob's Lucky Spot, the Rainbow Gardens, the Pumpkin Center Barn Dance, the Beardsley Ballroom, the Clover Club, and Tex's Barrel House.

Tommy Collins was an Oklahoman who moved to Bakersfield in 1951. He began writing songs for Ferlin Husky and played at the Blackboard. "The San Joaquin Valley, including Bakersfield, is where the people went during the Dust Bowl," Collins told journalist Dale Vinicur. "A lot of people from Oklahoma, Texas, Missouri, and Arkansas. Fresno is 105 miles north. It's still farm country, but the people from Oklahoma, Texas, Arkansas, Missouri went to the Bakersfield area. There's quite a history to the camaraderie that developed between those Dust Bowl people. They weren't apt to go for fancy music." Buck Owens was just one who came to the San Joaquin Valley from Texas. "I was part of the

above Country music in Lotus Land: steel guitarist Speedy West (second from left), Cliffie Stone (at microphone), and Tennessee Ernie Ford (center rear).

Grapes of Wrath migration," he said. "It started to the San Joaquin Valley because that's where the work was. The tomatoes and the 'taters and the grapes and the peaches. All the work. Every year, we'd make a foray, we'd come out here, we'd start in about May with the potatoes, and we'd go up to Porterville for the carrots, and so on. You know, you had to help the family."

The sound began with unheralded musicians such as Bill Woods, who had arrived at the Blackboard in 1950 after a stint on the road with Bob Wills' former vocalist, Tommy Duncan. Woods was a guitarist, and one of the first to figure out a role for the Telecaster in country music. He brought Ferlin Husky to Bakersfield, and Husky encouraged Tommy Collins to stay, and so the scene developed.

Down in Los Angeles, Cliffie Stone hosted live country music on KXLA, and, in 1948, launched a Saturday night barn dance, *Hometown Jamboree*, in El Monte. Stone managed Tennessee Ernie Ford and was especially tight with Capitol's Ken Nelson. Ford's producer, Lee Gillette, together with Nelson and Stone, organized a music publishing company, Central Songs. Gillette and Nelson kept quiet about their involvement, so Stone became the company figurehead. Nearly all the up-and-coming talent from the greater Los Angeles area appeared on Stone's KXLA show or on *Hometown Jamboree*, and if they showed any promise, he would sign them to Central Songs, then get them on Capitol Records. Stone helped Nelson to organize the sessions, and recruited a core of session men as deft and adaptable as any in Nashville. Steel guitarist Speedy West and lead guitarist Jimmy Bryant could cover all the bases from hillbilly waltzes to progressive jazz. "The Nashville Sound is the musicians," said Nelson. "The musicians are all fairly well trained; that is, they have studied music and they have a smoothness

about them. Bakersfield has a roughness about it because of their background, where they lived, where they came from. The other thing about Nashville is the musical vocal backgrounds. We used the Jordanaires in Nashville, which we never used in Bakersfield. Bakersfield had a roughness that was American." To a great extent, Stone and Nelson had Bakersfield sewn up. The only early Bakersfield classic they missed was Joe Maphis's "Dim Lights, Thick Smoke, and Loud Loud Music." Maphis wrote it right in the Blackboard Café.

Dim lights, thick smoke, and loud, loud music
Is the only kind of life you'll ever understand
Dim lights, thick smoke and loud, loud music
You'll never make a wife to a home-lovin' man

A home and little children mean nothing to you
A house filled with love and a husband so true
You'd rather have a drink with the first guy you meet
And the only home you'll know is the bar down the street

Out drinkin' and dancin' to a honky tonk band
Is the only kind of life you'll ever understand
Go out and have your fun, you think you've played it smart
I'm sorry for you and your honky tonk heart

Ken Nelson signed Tommy Collins to Capitol. He scored some hits with novelty songs such as "You Better Not Do That," "It Tickles," and "You Oughta See Pickles Now," but the real Bakersfield Sound was on songs such as "High on a Hilltop." In the latter, Collins loses his love to a smooth-talking rounder. She's "silly with booze," and alone on the hilltop he sees the devil in her. It was a record that almost poured itself a beer. The true-to-life blues. Before long, though, Collins became convinced that the devil was within himself.

That was the music Nashville was trying to leave behind. Merle Haggard later recorded "High on a

below Ray Price plays *The Opry*.
opposite Ray Price with Hank Williams' old band, featuring Don Helms on steel guitar.

Hilltop" and made Collins his in-house songwriter. The electric guitar threading its way through Collins' recordings was played by Alvis "Buck" Owens, and during the 1960s Owens became the poster boy for the Bakersfield Sound. Some even called it "Buckersfield." He played at the Blackboard from 1951 until 1958, and was signed to Capitol in 1957. Unfortunately, he arrived just as the rockabillies were dictating airplay, and had to wait two years for the pendulum to swing back. In late 1959, "Under Your Spell Again" reached number four on *Billboard*'s country charts, and from that point every one of Owens' records, with the exception of a few Christmas singles and one or two other novelties, reached the charts. Ken Nelson preferred singers to record their own songs with their own bands, and his creative latitude was essential to Owens' development. "He told me," Owens said later, "'What I tried to do was duck and burrow. I just stayed the hell out of your way.'" The classic Owens sound was high and hard-driving, tailored to counteract the small, muddy sound of car radios. "Back in the '30s, the jazz musicians would say, 'It don't mean a thing if it ain't got that swing,'" said Owens. "I say, 'It don't mean a thang if it ain't got that twang.'" He became the complete package. He wrote the songs, played lead guitar, effectively produced his own records, managed and booked himself, and understood the business. Buck Owens *really* understood the business. As soon as he could, he wrestled his music publishing away from Central Songs, and in 1980 he became the first country artist to gain control of his old recordings. "In Nashville," Owens concluded, "what they were doing was contagious. They wanted for it to have some chance to cross over so they could get some extra buyers. But I didn't make my records like that. I made the record, I made the songs, I wrote the songs I liked, I played them the way I liked. If somebody else liked them, hell yes. If they didn't, well, I'll make another one for you. Don't go no place, I'll make you something you like pretty soon."

It wasn't just the Bakersfield musicians who kept country music's traditional agenda and sound alive. Ray Price did not play rock 'n' roll. He kept his music rooted in the beerhalls, and, to the surprise of many, became more successful than ever. Price had made his first record for Bullet in 1950 and arrived in Nashville the following year. Early in 1952, he roomed with Hank Williams during the doomed singer's last year, and kept the Williams sound alive to the point of hiring his old band. After five years and half a dozen mostly minor hits, Price went to see Columbia's Don Law with a song he'd heard in Florida. It was a Bakersfield song—Kenny Brown and Marilyn Kay's "Crazy Arms." On March 1, 1956, with Elvis's "Heartbreak Hotel" closing in on number one, Price recorded "Crazy Arms." The traditional hillbilly sound was a plodding 2/4, but Price employed Brown and Kay's walking 4/4 shuffle rhythm. He added drums and Bakersfield-style harmony vocals on the bridge. "Crazy Arms" was an unusual

arrangement of an even more unusual song ("crazy arms that long to hold somebody new"), but it shot to the top of the country charts on June 23, 1956 and stayed there twenty weeks. Rock 'n' roll was ruling the airwaves, but no one had told Ray Price.

The hillbilly shuffle as popularized by Ray Price became the anti-Nashville Sound. "Wasted Words," "I've Got a New Heartache," "My Shoes Keep Walking Back to You," "Invitation to the Blues," "City Lights," and "Heartaches by the Number" were huge hits during the mid-to-late 1950s. Price's new band, the Cherokee Cowboys, wore headdresses and gaudy rhinestone-studded uniforms in stark contrast to the sartorial sobriety of the Nashville Sound artists. Price hired several up-and-coming young artists for his band, including Roger Miller (who wrote "Invitation to the Blues"),

Willie Nelson, and Johnny Paycheck. He spearheaded country music's first "back to the bar-rooms" movement. In his wake came Charlie Walker with several more classic hillbilly shuffles, including "Pick Me up on Your Way Down" and "Who Will Buy the Wine," and, after a failed career as a rock 'n' roller, Faron Young returned to hardcore country music with songs such as "Alone with You" and "That's the Way I Feel."

The Nashville Sound slowly morphed into today's country music, but the country shuffle became the touchstone of the alternative country movement. Price himself forsook it in 1967, switching abruptly to string-laden ballads as he reinvented himself as a country supper-club act, but in later years he too realized that he'll be remembered for the shuffles, not the strings.

Chapter 12

HONKY-TONK *Angels*

Around 2:00 PM on Tuesday March 5, 1963, three passengers and a pilot boarded a Piper Comanche light airplane in Kansas City bound for Nashville. They touched down in Dyersburg, Tennessee, around 5:00, refueled, and took off again at 6:07. The weather was bad, but the pilot wanted to get home, and so did everyone else on board.

Bad weather had already delayed them by one day, so they decided to take their chances. One hour out of Dyersburg, a rainstorm and encroaching darkness disoriented the pilot and he crashed the plane into dense woods near Camden, Tennessee, less than 100 miles from Nashville. All four on board were killed.

Patsy Cline, Cowboy Copas, Hawkshaw Hawkins, and the pilot, Randy Hughes, were the four killed. Hughes, once a musician himself, was Copas's son-in-law and Patsy Cline's manager/paramour. Hawkshaw Hawkins was a tall, genial country singer who had given up a seat on a commercial flight so that his *Opry* co-star Billy Walker could rush back to be with his ailing father. They had all been in Kansas City to perform at a benefit show for the family of a disc-jockey who had died five weeks earlier in a car wreck. Cowboy Copas and Hawkshaw Hawkins had been stars since the 1940s, but had faded with time. Quite the opposite was the case with Patsy Cline. Death magnified her stardom. Her work came to suggest a very modern mixture of vulnerability and resilience.

Traditionally, country music had been a male-dominated profession. In its pre-history, women were primarily responsible for handing down songs from

above Patsy Cline.
opposite Patsy Cline holds court in Nashville shortly before her death.

above and right The Maddox Brothers & Rose—the Most Colorful Hillbilly Band in America.

generation to generation, but at the dawn of the country music business there was no escaping the male bias. The songs mirrored that bias. Several commentators tried to find neo-feminism in the Carter Family's "Single Girl, Married Girl," which drew an unflattering comparison between the barefoot and pregnant married girl and the fancy-free single girl, but the song was something of an aberration. Far more Carter Family songs featured women as abandoned lovers and widowed wives, and when Sara Carter divorced A. P., it was hushed up so that the Carter Family could still appear as the family that prayed together and stayed together.

The first female country star was Patsy Montana. Born in Arkansas, she reinvented herself in Chicago as a singing cowgirl, and recorded her landmark song, "I Want to Be a Cowboy's Sweetheart," in 1935. It was an unremarkable record in many ways, but its blitheness and escapism persuaded more than 1 million people to pay 75 cents for it at the height of the Depression, thus making it the first million-selling record by a female country singer. The message was subtly different from the Carter Family's message:

Patsy Montana wanted to ride the range alongside her sweetheart, not cook bacon and biscuits and wait at the bunkhouse door for his return.

Newfound freedoms afforded women during the Second World War found a subtle reflection in country music. Rose Maddox fronted a family band, and looked and acted as if she could take care of herself in a bar-room brawl. The Maddoxes moved from Alabama to the west coast, and dubbed themselves "The Maddox Brothers & Rose—the Most Colorful Hillbilly Band in America." They played loud and fast, building sight gags and magic into their act. Their repertoire included some roguish honky-tonk songs that practically reeked of beer, puke and smoke ("Hangover Blues," "Ugly and Slouchy," "Honky Tonkin'," and a cover version of Ruth Brown's R&B hit, "Wild, Wild Young Men"), but the Maddoxes recorded far more folk songs, religious songs, and traditional country numbers. And none of their records was a really big hit.

Country music was never quite ready for them.

The biggest country record by a female singer during the 1950s was Kitty Wells' "It Wasn't God Who Made Honky Tonk Angels." Not only was it written by a man, but it was written by a man sniffing out an easy buck. J. D. Miller later produced wonderful swamp blues records by the likes of Lightnin' Slim and Slim Harpo, but in 1951 he was hustling his way in the country music business. He realized that the melody of Hank Thompson's big hit "Wild Side of Life" was in the public domain, so he wouldn't have to share the copyright on an answer-song with the writers of Thompson's record (in fact, the melody had come from England several hundred years earlier, and had already been used by the Carter Family on "I'm Thinking Tonight of My Blue Eyes"). Inspiration and greed struck Miller on

Route 90 in Louisiana, and he pulled his car over and scribbled down his sequel. He didn't know it, but his lyrics would strike a chord with millions of women, especially the lines "Too many times married men think they're still single / That has caused many a good girl to go wrong." Miller owned a tiny label called Feature Records, and got a local singer, Alice Montgomery, to record it. Miller then placed the song with Fred Rose at Acuff-Rose, who persuaded Decca's Paul Cohen to record a version with Kitty Wells. Little known at the time, Kitty Wells didn't cut the song because she empathized with the lyrics, but because she needed the session fee. She was never a honky-tonk angel. She wore gingham dresses buttoned to the neck and falling well below the knees. She was demure and tightlipped, and always deferred to her

husband, Johnnie Wright of the duo Johnnie and Jack.

Kitty Wells seems to have had very little influence on Patsy Cline. Patsy was sixteen when she made her radio debut on a local station in Winchester, Virginia, and soon began performing at beerhalls and lodges. She probably adopted the name "Patsy" in honor of Patsy Montana, and in 1953 she married a local housebuilder named Gerald Cline. They divorced in 1956, but by then Ginny Hensley was Patsy Cline. In 1954, she signed her first recording contract with 4-Star Records in Pasadena, California. Its president, Bill McCall, had already figured out that the real money in the record business was in publishing, and he made a point of buying songs from down-on-their-luck hillbilly singers. In this way, he acquired "Release Me" and several other valuable copyrights. He usually appeared in the composer credits as "W. S. Stevenson" (a contraction of his two favorite writers, Robert Louis Stevenson and William

Shakespeare). Right around the time that he signed Patsy Cline, McCall got out of the record business and leased several of his artists to Decca Records with the stipulation that they record only 4-Star songs. McCall's tactic severely limited Patsy Cline's choice of songs and placed a six-year roadblock in her career. She got only one truly great song from 4-Star—"Walking after Midnight." When her contract expired in November 1960, she signed directly with Decca, forging a close working relationship with the company's Nashville chief, Owen Bradley.

Kitty Wells wasn't going to steal anyone's husband or dance on tabletops, and she certainly wasn't going to rock or roll. Patsy Cline was altogether different. She could sing straightahead country music and she could sing rock 'n' roll, but it was only after she signed with Decca that she discovered her true voice. She loved early 1950s' pop singers, such as Patti Page and Jo Stafford, and began phrasing country songs as if they were pop songs. She sang languorously, but with the authority of a mature woman, and as her music changed, so did her look. She began her career in cowgirl outfits, but soon switched to sheath dresses, silver fox stoles, and stiletto heels, forever changing the look of women in country music.

Patsy Cline was hitting her stride at the time of her death. The moody, ethereal "Walkin' after Midnight" had been a major hit in 1957, but it was followed by a long, dry spell before "I Fall to Pieces" topped the country charts in August 1961. Nineteen months later, she was dead. As if to underscore the difference between a star and a legend, Patsy Cline scored just nine hits during her lifetime. She wasn't

above Patsy Montana.
opposite Never a honky-tonk angel. Kitty Wells, demure singer and dedicated housewife, at home with her husband Johnnie Wright.

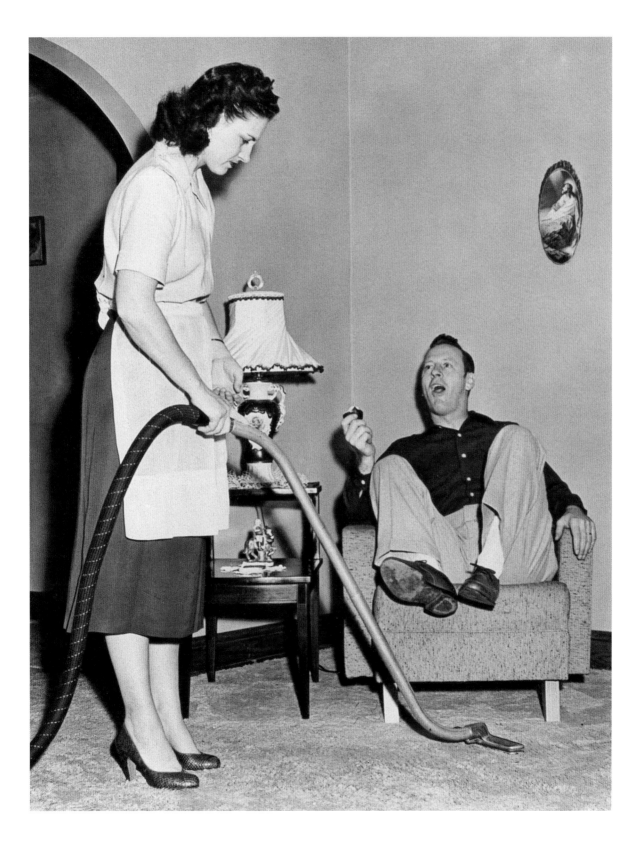

a big star, but became a legend. Her style has so colored country music that few women country singers tackle a ballad without making at least an indirect reference to her.

Several female singers claim that Patsy Cline mentored them, none more so than Loretta Lynn. The broad strokes of Lynn's story are well known. She has made her ascent from rural privation to the top of the charts into a piece of American folklore. She serialized her story in countless songs and a best-selling autobiography, *Coal Miner's Daughter*, which in turn became a top-grossing movie. Whether going station to station with her first record or appearing on network talk shows, Loretta Lynn has been an aggressive self-promoter, but her story resonated with many women. She grew up in the coal-mining area of Kentucky and was married at age thirteen to Mooney Lynn. By the time she was eighteen, she had four children, and Mooney

had moved his young family to Washington State. He told people that his wife sang better than anyone he'd ever heard, except Kitty Wells, and he found a believer at the tiny Zero Records in Vancouver, Canada. Loretta cut her first record, "I'm a Honky Tonk Girl," in Los Angeles with Ken Nelson's crew, then hit the road promoting it.. The song suggested Kitty Wells, right down to the tremulous vibrato, but on subsequent singles she became more assertive. Loretta and Mooney arrived in Nashville in September 1960, and her contract was acquired by Owen Bradley at Decca Records. There were a few halting steps, but Loretta Lynn found that the more she drew upon her own life, the more her records sold. Her singles mixed feisty humor with blue-collar pride, and an almost-feminist agenda. "You Ain't Woman Enough to Take My Man," "Don't Come a Drinkin' (with Lovin' on Your Mind)," "Fist City," "Your Squaw Is on the

Warpath," "One's on the Way," and "The Pill" were a world apart from Kitty Wells' hushed lamentations. It was hard to believe that just a decade separated them.

Sheer force of personality worked for Dolly Parton, too. The contradictions in her say much about country music itself. She deserves to be taken seriously (royalties from just one of her songs, "I Will Always Love You," exceed the gross domestic product of some smaller countries), but she won't take herself too seriously. There's a dark and solemn side to her music that harks back to country music's prehistory, but it's offset by her bouffants, sequin pantsuits, and rhinestones. She'll act like she's just ridden into town on a mule, but can look over a contract with the finesse of a lawyer. And her grown woman's songs are often sung with childlike vulnerability.

Dolly Parton arrived in Nashville from east Tennessee immediately after she got out of school in 1964. She wrote a couple of minor hits for other artists, then starred on Porter Wagoner's television show. In 1967, Wagoner persuaded Chet Atkins that Dolly Parton belonged on RCA. The true nature of the relationship between Porter Wagoner and Dolly Parton is one of the great unknowables in

country music, but Wagoner surely taught her to be unafraid of making a splash. Her outfits grew increasingly outlandish, like Mae West gone country, and, like Mae West, Dolly Parton portrayed female sexuality in a more daring way by appearing to lampoon it. The outfits and wigs were part of a broader strategy. They got her noticed, and, once noticed, she had a song to sell. Perhaps they were also a mask, and without them the real Dolly Parton could be herself. On some level she might have craved anonymity as much as her notoriously unphotographed husband.

There are recurring themes in Dolly Parton's songs: home; the preciousness of childhood memories; optimism in the face of any adversity; and the quest for love wherever it may be found. Like Loretta Lynn, she was unafraid of broaching taboos. One of her early hits, "Just Because I'm a Woman," tackled a double standard that it was all right for men to be sexually experienced on the wedding night, but not women. She mined her own background for songs of fierce Appalachian pride, such as "Coat of Many Colors," "In the Good Old Days (When Times Were Bad)," "Tennessee Homesick Blues," and "My Tennessee Mountain Home." And, like Porter Wagoner, she was unafraid to tackle the subject of mental illness ("Daddy Come and Get Me").

Ten years after Porter Wagoner became her manager, producer, and costar, Dolly Parton left him and hired a new manager, Sandy Gallin, in Los Angeles. Gallin managed Cher and Joan Rivers, and reshaped Dolly Parton's career. It's a mark of his success that for a few years she was omnipresent. There were profiles in *People* magazine and *Good Housekeeping*, even the cover of *Playboy*. There was television, television, and more television, a European tour, and Vegas. And, of course, there

was griping in Nashville, but Dolly Parton paid it no mind. "I'm not leaving country music," she insisted. "All I want is a chance to do everything I want to do in life." Her first movie, *Nine to Five*, was one of the top-grossing films of 1981. She wrote the title song, and it became a number one pop hit. And then, as her career cooled, Whitney Houston recorded her farewell to Porter Wagoner, "I Will Always Love You," and it became one of the best-selling songs of the 1990s. With the financial security afforded by that song, Dolly returned to her first love, bluegrass music, and once again proved to be ahead of the game.

While Dolly Parton and Loretta Lynn always seemed self-directed, and totally in control of their lives and careers, Tammy Wynette seemed cruelly buffeted by both. Her life was as exaggerated as a soap opera. When she was nine months old, her father, William Pugh, died of an inoperable brain tumor. He had sung and played guitar with a family hillbilly band, but gave up his ambitions to raise his family. He left a battered, privately recorded disc, but by the time Tammy was able to ask the engineers at Columbia Records to transfer it, it was unplayable. After her father's death, she lived with her grandparents on a cotton farm. Married at eighteen, she was a mother at nineteen and again at twenty. Pregnant with her third child, she left her first husband, enrolled in a beauty school and worked in a bar. She moved to Birmingham, Alabama, where one of her uncles was an engineer on a local television station. He got her a job as a girl singer on the early morning show, and before long, people began telling her that she should go to Nashville. In January 1966, she packed everything she owned in the trunk of her car, put her kids in

opposite Bluegrass when bluegrass wasn't cool—Dolly Parton.

the back seat, and drove to Nashville. The first offer came from Billy Sherrill at Epic Records. "I was impressed with her voice," Sherrill said later. "It had this cry in it that really got to you." It was the sound of the woman for whom nothing would ever go right. Inspired by the Debbie Reynolds movie *Tammy and the Bachelor*, Sherrill renamed his new singer Tammy Wynette, and, faced with a dearth of good material for women, he began writing songs for her. Many of them had a wounded innocence and a soap opera-like theatricality. Her first big hit, "My Elusive Dreams," was a duet with Sherrill's other major act, David Houston. It was the story of a couple who chase their dreams across the country. "We didn't find it there, so we moved on."

By the fourth single, "I Don't Wanna Play House," Tammy Wynette was staking out her own ground. The song looked at divorce through the eyes of a child, and it became her first solo number one hit. Loretta Lynn remembered thinking, "I got some competition here." Sherrill looked for songs that dealt with the nuts and bolts of everyday life, and when he couldn't find them, he wrote them. "Take Me to Your World" was a barmaid's prayer for deliverance from honky-tonks and dirty jokes. "The Ways to Love a Man" and "They Call it Making Love" tackled sexuality in ways that would have made Kitty Wells blush. "D-I-V-O-R-C-E," "Bedtime Story," and "Kids Say the Darndest Things" confronted the agony of divorce and the effect it had on children. Then, two years into her recording career, Tammy Wynette cut her anthem.

Billy Sherrill had been nursing the title "Stand by Your Man" for several months, but hadn't done anything with it. Then, as Tammy remembered, "We had gone in to record a three-hour session, and we had recorded two songs, and there was nothing else that anybody had brought in that we

liked. Billy said to the musicians, 'Okay, take a break.' We went upstairs to his office, and he said, 'I have an idea,' and we wrote 'Stand by Your Man' in twenty minutes." Sherrill, a true musical ecletic who had begun his career in R&B bands and loved Johann Strauss more than Hank Williams, adapted the melody from a Strauss waltz. Tammy Wynette gave the performance of her life. The final climactic notes made the song into a trailer park "My Way." There was no doubt that it would go over well in deeply conservative areas of the South, but it became a surprise top twenty pop hit as well, and the fact that it sold 5 million copies suggested that feminism still had some converts to make.

Ironically, "Stand by Your Man" was recorded just as Tammy had decided not to stand beside her man…for the second time. Shortly after arriving in Nashville, she'd married songwriter Don Chapel, but left him to move in with her idol, George Jones. In a scene worthy of a soap opera, Jones literally took Tammy away from Chapel. It was a dramatic beginning to a highly charged relationship. On the surface, it looked like a fairytale romance. George adopted Tammy's three daughters, and they had another of their own, Tamala Georgette. They bought a sprawling nineteenth-century mansion in Lakeland, Florida, and erected a country music park on the grounds. "We had captured [the public's] imagination in a special way," Tammy wrote in her autobiography. "George was a legend, the king, who had romantically run off with his queen, sired a beautiful princess, and was now living happily ever after." But this was George Jones and Tammy Wynette, so "happily ever after" was not an option. The book went on to chronicle in harrowing detail her mounting despair, then fearfulness over Jones' drinking, violence, and bouts of uncontrollable behavior.

Tammy Wynette divorced Jones in 1975, and if those years had not been turbulent enough, worse was to follow. There were mysterious break-ins, daubed death threats, arsons at her home, and a reported abduction that has never been explained. Within fifteen months she had surgery three times and was hospitalized another five times with complications. Her grandmother, who'd raised her, died in 1976, and her grandfather was incapacitated by a stroke. A well-publicized affair with Burt Reynolds was splashed over the tabloids, and a fourth marriage to a Nashville real estate broker was over before the confetti had been cleared away. Then, in July 1978, she married producer George Richey, and they stayed together until her death. Her recording career faltered, but had one last, sweet

opposite Tammy Wynette.
below Tammy Wynette in the studio with George Jones and their producer, Billy Sherrill.

coda. Statistically at least, the biggest hit of her career came in 1991 when she and a Scottish band, the KLF (Kopyright Liberation Front), recorded "Justified and Ancient." It was high techno-camp and soared to number eleven in the American pop charts, and to number one in eighteen other countries. "It was done for all the right reasons," she said later. "For fun, and for a change."

Tammy Wynette died in her sleep home on April 6, 1998. She was 55. It was an uncommonly peaceful end to a turbulent life, but her children later called for exhumation and made dark allegations of foul play. Unlike Dolly Parton or Loretta Lynn, Tammy Wynette wrote few of her songs, but she chose material that reflected a generation making its awkward way through adulthood, dealing with social upheavals and changing gender roles. She might not have stood by her men, but she gave voice to those who did.

Chapter 13

TO THE BRINK
and Back

Johnny Cash and George Jones are almost exact contemporaries and began recording within months of each other. Both saw rock 'n' roll derail their young careers, both battled life-threatening addictions, and both suffered at the hands of the press. They survived to become the biggest country stars of the 1960s and 1970s, but always remained Nashville outsiders.

The similarity ends there. George Jones is a singer's singer. Nearly every major country star has gone on record as saying that Jones is the gold standard of country singing. Cash, on the other hand, has a painfully small vocal range that invited parody and derision when he started. The differences run deeper. Cash is pensive to a fault. He is a self-taught man who has never tired of learning, and has hawked his conscience from cause to cause, unafraid of championing unpopular agendas. He thinks, he feels, he talks. George Jones remains inscrutable. His utterances are mostly empty or platitudinous, leaving you wondering if he is excessively diplomatic or if his only means of expressing anything of consequence is through a song. And whereas Cash usually brought an inordinate amount of consideration to his work, Jones often applied his gift to songs of unutterable stupidity.

A name could be no plainer than George Jones. His family lived in Saratoga, Texas, an oil boom town that had gone bust before the Depression. It was in a bedeviled area of east Texas dubbed "Big Thicket." The bush was thick, the humidity was stifling, and there were snakes, mosquitoes, marshes, and

above George Jones.
opposite Johnny Cash, TV star, 1969.

#6-JC-69
TAPE DATE: 4/16/69
AIR DATE: 7/12/69
THE JOHNNY CASH SHOW

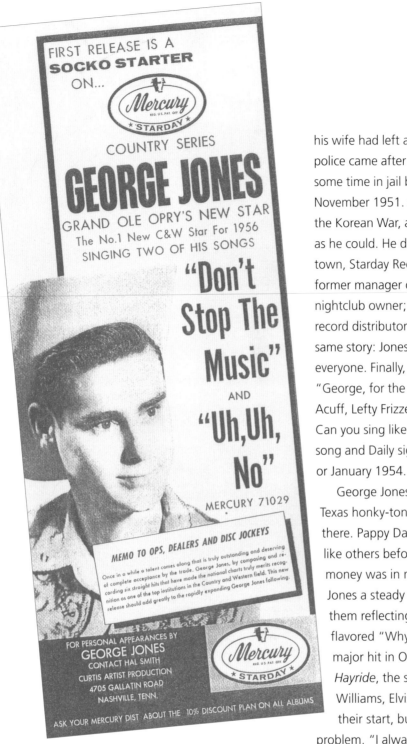

his wife had left and he was working the joints. The police came after him for non-support, and he spent some time in jail before joining the Marines in November 1951. Stationed in California, he avoided the Korean War, and returned to Beaumont as soon as he could. He discovered a new record company in town, Starday Records. "Star-" was Jack Starnes, a former manager of Lefty Frizzell and a local nightclub owner; "-day" was "Pappy" Daily, a record distributor in Houston. Daily always told the same story: Jones began his first session by imitating everyone. Finally, in desperation, Daily said, "George, for the last few hours you've sung like Roy Acuff, Lefty Frizzell, Hank Williams, and Bill Monroe. Can you sing like George Jones?" Jones did another song and Daily signed him. It was December 1953 or January 1954.

George Jones' sound was rooted in the east Texas honky-tonks, and for many years it remained there. Pappy Daily became his producer, and Daily, like others before him, realized that the real money was in music publishing. He fed George Jones a steady diet of songs he owned, most of them reflecting his east Texas bias. The Cajun-flavored "Why, Baby, Why" became Jones' first major hit in October 1955. He joined *Louisiana Hayride*, the show that had given Hank Williams, Elvis, Johnny Cash, and Jim Reeves their start, but his drinking was already a problem. "I always hated my daddy for drinking," he said in a rare moment of candor, "and I didn't drink as a kid. [In] the dives and the honky-tonks the drunks were always blowing foul breath in my face, and the smell of whiskey was enough to knock you out if you hadn't had a few yourself. Drinking gives me courage. I'm easily depressed. I can feel it creeping up, and the best way to simmer down is with a drink."

swamps. Malaria took the life of George's oldest sister five years before he was born. George Jones grew up in Beaumont, and there's an often-published photo of him walking the streets of the town aged twelve or thirteen, playing his guitar. He looks resolute in his choice of profession.

George Jones married in 1950 and tried to hold down a day job as a laborer, but, before too long,

When rock 'n' roll broke, George Jones became "Thumper" Jones for one single, "How Come It, Dad Gummit," then reverted to honky-tonk music. "It was in there too deep," he said. "I did some rock, had fun with it, but it didn't touch my heart. I was always looking forward to the next song so I could get back to a ballad." He joined *The Grand Ole Opry* on August 4, 1956, one month after Johnny Cash, but didn't move to Nashville. His biggest hit during the 1950s came with a song that was equal parts honky-tonk and rockabilly, "White Lightning." Jones hee-hawed it up in a giddy, bibulous frenzy. He could have gone with the Nashville Sound, but stayed on his home turf. "The Window up Above," "Color of the Blues," "Accidentally on Purpose," "She Thinks I Still Care" were pure, hardcore country: a stiff corrective to the Nashville Sound. Jones himself wrote "The Window up Above," but couldn't explain where it came from. It just floated into his life one morning, and seemed to reflect the disquiet he found behind every domestic scene. Occasionally, he'd turn to songs that caught the drinker's morning-after desolation, such as "Warm Red Wine," "You're Still on My Mind," "Just One More," or "Out of Control." He sang them as if they were backslider's prayers, and the results were as heartwrenching as anything in country music.

But Jones and Daily had no quality control. If Daily published it, he liked it. If Daily liked it, George Jones would record it. For every song like "Things Have Gone to Pieces" or "A Girl I Used to Know," there were others like "Eskimo Pie" or "The Poor Chinee" ("Me likee bow-wow, very good chow-chow"). The lack of quality control seemed to imply that Jones didn't care. Then, in

1971, he broke with Daily to sign with Epic Records, thus joining his third wife, Tammy Wynette. He finally moved to Nashville and drew songs from the Nashville song mill. At best, the results were stunning. "The Grand Tour," "The Door," and, of course, "He Stopped Loving Her Today." The last of these is often cited as the greatest country record ever made. The production was deliriously over the top, but the song was of love so obsessive it could end only in death. And death seemed the likeliest outcome for George Jones in the years after his 1975 divorce from Wynette. He grew addicted to cocaine, no-showed to the point that bookers wouldn't touch him, even became homeless for a while. Wynette insisted that he stalked her. After a fourth marriage to Nancy

above George Jones with his producer, Pappy Daily.

Sepulvado in March 1983, he seemed to stabilize. "All my life I've been running from something," he told United Press in 1984. "If I knew what it was, maybe I could run in the right direction." His songs, the best of them at least, tell us about the dark places and about the shame of doing wrong. He provided a soundtrack for other peoples' lives, while only halfway in control of his own.

Johnny Cash arrived at the door of Sun Records in Memphis six or eight months after Elvis Presley, and with a sound that remained essentially unchanged. His dry humor would surface occasionally, but he knew that his baritone was better suited to songs of loss, alienation, and grief. Originally from rural Arkansas, Cash was twenty-three years old, just out of the air force and newly married, when he arrived at Sun. He hoped to become a radio announcer, but couldn't shake the idea of becoming a singer. Like Elvis, he probably hadn't performed professionally when he auditioned, but nevertheless arrived with a fully realized vision of his music. His early sessions included folk songs, country songs, and gospel, with an occasional novelty song for light relief. The menu wouldn't change much. His voice was framed by the minimal, often ragged, backing of the Tennessee Two. Sun Records wasn't in Nashville, and Sun president Sam Phillips didn't make Nashville records. He was starting to see good sales of Elvis Presley, who recorded with just an electric guitar, string bass, and acoustic guitar. Phillips decided that Johnny Cash's voice needed no more ornamentation than that. "Can you hear Johnny Cash with a steel guitar?" he asked. Every Nashville producer would have replied, "Yes." "Nashville in 1955 was grinding out all these country records," said Cash, "and if you took the voice off, all the tracks sounded the same. It's kinda that way with my music, but at least it's my music."

Cash's first Sun record, "Cry! Cry! Cry!" entered the national country charts just weeks after George Jones' debut. He followed it with "Folsom Prison Blues," a song derived from a Gordon Jenkins record, "Crescent City Blues." Jenkins arranged many of the Weavers' biggest hits and directed early concept LPs, such as *Manhattan Tower*, and Cash has never explained why he thought he could take one of Jenkins' songs, change a few words, and call it his own. With rock 'n' roll on the near horizon, he tried writing a song or two for Elvis,

then wrote another rockabilly song, "Rock 'n' roll Ruby," which he pitched to fellow Sun act Warren Smith. Yet another rockabilly song, "You're My Baby" (originally "Little Woolly Booger"), went to Roy Orbison, who was also recording for Sun at the time. But Cash, like George Jones, realized that rock 'n' roll wasn't for him. He followed "Folsom Prison Blues" with a strikingly hypnotic and original song, "I Walk the Line." It was a pledge of love to his young wife, Vivian Liberto Cash, arranged in such a way that it changed key after every verse. Cash telegraphed the modulation with a two-bar hum. The chord pattern was unusual, inspired by hearing a tape played backward. Guitarist Luther Perkins walked up and down the bass strings while Cash played rhythm guitar with paper threaded through the strings for a percussive effect. Released at the dawn of rock 'n' roll era, it topped the country charts and reached number seventeen on the pop charts. No more unusual country record has ever been made.

Trying to bring variety to Cash's formula, Phillips recruited another producer, Jack Clement, who fed Cash a steady diet of teen operettas he'd composed, framing them with bright and breezy pop arrangements. Statistically, Clement's "Ballad of a Teenage Queen" was Cash's biggest hit on Sun, but it was one that Cash rarely if ever sang after its day had passed. He left Sun when his three-year contract was up in 1958. Columbia's Don Law saw him as a long-term artist. "It's the virility and guts to his voice that he's got," said Law. "He's always sung off-pitch, but he can just walk out and say, 'I'm Johnny Cash.'" Law, though, found that he couldn't re-create the tightly focused

opposite Johnny Cash plays *The Grand Ole Opry*, 1956, with Marshall Grant (left) and Luther Perkins (right).

Sun tape echo. The early Columbia recordings sounded empty and cavernous, which was doubly unfortunate because Cash had been saving some of his best songs for Columbia—"I Still Miss Someone," "Don't Take Your Guns to Town," and "Five Feet High and Rising." Very soon, though, Law needed the echo to disguise Cash's chronic hoarseness and shrunken vocal range, both resulting from an increasing dependency on amphetamines.

Soon after signing with Columbia, Cash left Memphis and *The Grand Ole Opry*, and moved to California. He hoped to expand his career into movies, but the only roles he could get were in sub-B movies, such as *Door to Door Maniac* and *Five Minutes to Live*. His Columbia contract called for two LPs a year, and Cash was among the first to do something creative with the country LP. The country market was singles-driven well into the 1970s. As Mercury Records' Nashville chief Jerry Kennedy said, "If you cut a hit, it was like a bummer because you'd have to find songs enough for an album. The sales weren't there. Six, eight, nine thousand copies wasn't bad."

Cash's first LPs were random collections of songs, but he soon turned LPs into conceptual pieces, like his collection of songs about Native Americans, *Bitter Tears*, and his western suite, *Ballads of the True West*. "He had an unquenchable desire for knowledge," said his manager, Saul Holiff. "He soaked up everything he needed to know, and, no matter what state he was in, he could pull a project together." When Don Law suggested the album of western songs, Cash didn't warm over "I've Got Spurs That Jingle, Jangle, Jingle," but drove into the desert for days, trying to imagine the

pioneer life. Unlike any other country albums, his albums sold, routinely exceeding 100,000 copies.

Cash also seemed able to get a hit when he really needed one, and to bring himself back from the brink when those around him were despairing. By 1963, he hadn't seen a top five country hit for three years, but then, in a dream, he heard Anita Carter's new single, "Love's Ring of Fire," with mariachi horns. Carter was the daughter of Mother Maybelle Carter, and the sister of Cash's future wife, June Carter. "Love's Ring of Fire" was a song that June had cowritten, and Cash recorded it as "Ring of Fire" with the horns in March 1963. It was daringly innovative and topped the country charts in July.

In 1964, Cash appeared at the Newport Folk Festival, and began aligning himself with the protest movement. "Johnny Cash, the Nashville star, closed the gap between commercial country and folk music with a masterly set of storytelling songs," wrote the influential *New York Times* critic Robert Shelton. Many in Nashville thought that Cash was actually drawing a line between himself and country music rather than closing the gap between country and folk. Cash, though, didn't care. He took out an advertisement in *Billboard*, castigating country radio for its cowardice in not playing his version of "The Ballad of Ira Hayes," and began a dialog with Bob Dylan, intoxicated by the lyrical freedoms Dylan had just handed him. When Ren Grevatt interviewed him for *Music Business* magazine in 1965, Cash made a point of saying that he'd been up all night singing with Bob Dylan. "I don't think anyone around today has so much to offer as him," he said. If anyone else in Nashville thought that way, they were keeping very quiet about it.

In October 1965, Cash was busted for bringing dexedrine tablets across the border from Mexico, and spent a night or so in jail. That year, he

opposite "Hello, I'm Johnny Cash."

separated from his wife and moved to Nashville. He wooed and eventually married June Carter, and began the slow process of turning his life around. He recorded two prison albums, *At Folsom Prison* and *At San Quentin*, and the latter topped the pop LP charts in 1969. His top-rated ABC-TV show started that year and ran until 1971. For several years, Cash was one of the biggest acts in American entertainment. There was something unutterably compelling about the sight of Johnny Cash at the microphone. The nervous tics, the grimaces, and the way every word seemed to have been thought of just that instant. He dominated every stage.

Columbia Records dropped Johnny Cash in 1986, and some lackluster albums he made for Mercury seemed to suggest that he'd finally run dry. But in another act of spectacular career regeneration he returned on the rap label, American Records, in 1994 with an album titled *American Recordings*. Accompanied by just his guitar, he sang old songs, new songs, gospel songs, with an occasional novelty number. It was much the same mix he'd brought to Sun almost forty years earlier, but stripped even of the barebones backing he'd used then. Stars, he seemed to be saying, are a dime-a-dozen; greatness is something else again.

Chapter 14

What Condition MY CONDITION *Was In*

Johnny Cash's fascination with country music's traditional folk roots deepened after he married into the Carter family, but at the same time he became the first to embrace the lyrical freedoms and social agenda of the progressive folk singers. His albums took risks that no other country albums had taken.

Other performers, such as Bobby Bare and Waylon Jennings, followed cautiously in his wake, covering some of folk music's more melodic and less contentious new songs (Ian & Sylvia's "Four Strong Winds" and Gordon Lightfoot's "Early Morning Rain"), but no one put themselves on the line as Cash did. At a time when country music's innate conservatism was never more apparent, he alone welcomed change. During the mid-1960s the turmoil in the world seemed to mirror the ever-present turmoil in his head. On many levels, he was as deeply conservative as anyone in country music, but he also saw the new opportunities. Cash aside, Bob Dylan's epic mid-1960s' albums and the British Invasion made little impact on country music. Honky-tonk veteran Moon Mullican recorded "I Ain't No Beatle (But I Want to Hold Your Hand)," and the comprehension of what was happening didn't run much deeper than that.

Roger Miller had come to Nashville in 1957 intent on doing whatever it took—songwriting or slogging it out on the road as a sideman—to work in music. He wrote hits for Ray Price, Jim Reeves, Ernest Tubb, and Faron Young, and recorded for one label after another without much success. By 1964, he had decided to go to Los Angeles and was looking for relocation money when

above Grammy time: Roger Miller and Jeannie C. Riley ("Harper Valley PTA").
opposite Kris Kristofferson.

opposite Glen Campbell with John Hartford, composer of "Gentle on My Mind."

producer Jerry Kennedy promised him an advance of $100 a song to do an album for Mercury. Miller had turned his back on Nashville, and finally gave vent to the surreal humor and offbeat phrasing that he'd kept under wraps for seven years. The first single from the Mercury album, "Dang Me," became a campus favorite, then tore up the country charts. It was followed by "Chug-a-Lug," "King of the Road," "Kansas City Star," "England Swings," and the more serious "Husbands and Wives." Dylan probably hadn't influenced Roger Miller, but Dylan had probably influenced Mercury to take a chance on something offbeat. For several years, Miller made wildly eccentric music, and appeared frequently on television, singing and talking in an amphetamine-fueled rush. He earned eleven Grammies in 1965 and 1966, but by 1968 he was unable to write. Hard as he tried, the songs wouldn't come.

For all his success, Roger Miller influenced almost no one. Kris Kristofferson, on the other hand, reshaped country songcraft. No one since Hank Williams had such a profound effect on the way songs were written in Nashville. He understood country music's melodicism and melodrama as deeply as he understood the romantic poets' sensibilities. He brought a new candor and emotional honesty to country music when change was needed. His gruff whiskey baritone never won many fans at country radio, but for the best part of a decade his songs were everywhere. Kristofferson was the son of a career military man. After the Second World War, Kristofferson, Sr. became head of air operations with the Arabian-American Oil Co. in Saudi Arabia, and sent his son to private school in southern California. Kristofferson won a Rhodes

scholarship to Oxford University in England, and got into the music business there. "I signed with this guy who had started Tommy Steele," he said. "He got me a record contract and billed me as 'The Yank from Oxford.'"

Returning to the United States, Kristofferson joined the Air Force, but quit in 1964 to try his luck in Nashville. He was a janitor at the Columbia Records studio, and, when funds ran short, ferried oil workers to the Gulf of Mexico. Then, in 1969, he suddenly became the most in-demand songwriter in town. Johnny Cash recorded "Sunday Morning Coming Down," Roger Miller (by now dependent on others) was the first to record "Me and Bobbie McGee," and Ray Price forsook the country shuffles to cut a string-laden version of "For the Good Times." Jerry Lee Lewis, who had only recently reinvented himself as a country singer, took "Once More with Feeling" into the charts, but Kristofferson's greatest success came in 1971 with "Help Me Make It Through the Night." It was inspired by a magazine article in which Frank Sinatra talked about needing a bottle or a woman to help him make it through the night, although, ironically, Sinatra was one of the few not to record it. Kristofferson's disarmingly humble reflection on his success, "Why Me?" became one of the few records he charted himself.

Quite suddenly, every songwriter in Nashville tried to become a sensitive new-age man. The results were generally dire. Honky-tonk queen Wanda Jackson recorded a song called "Everything Is Leaving," and her discomfort was almost palpable as she stumbled through lines such as "old memories are flying, expanding pressures to my thinking." Only Mickey Newbury and one or two others approximated what Kristofferson was doing. Signed to Acuff-Rose, Newbury began writing straightahead country songs, but scored

his first hit when Kenny Rogers recorded "Just Dropped in to See What Condition My Condition Was in." Newbury was neither as prolific nor as successful as Kristofferson. His songs "Sweet Memories," "She Even Woke Me up to Say Goodbye," and "Here Comes the Rain, Baby" seemed drawn from the melancholy that blighted his life. His biggest hit, "American Trilogy," was a montage of "Dixie," "All My Trials," and "Battle Hymn of the Republic." When Newbury recorded it in 1971, the intent seemed almost ironic, but when Elvis Presley recorded it the following year, it became the exultation of the patriot and the self-made man.

Kristofferson's songs, Cash's gritty charisma, and Roger Miller's surreality gave country music its biggest breakthrough since the dawn of the Nashville Sound, but in commercial terms Glen Campbell dwarfed them all. In 1968, Campbell outsold the Beatles, although in fairness it should be pointed out that Capitol released or re-released six Glen Campbell albums that year, while the Beatles released just one, *The White Album*, and that at year's end. Campbell always deflected criticism from within country music by insisting that he was a "country boy who sang, not a country singer," but he arrived when country music was in need of direction, and he broke the three-chord barrier. He brought a new audience to country music, an audience made up for the greater part of people who would have said they didn't like country music, and *that* was the market that Nashville wanted.

Campbell had been a teenage country prodigy, a hugely in-demand session guitarist, a folk singer, and a Beach Boy. He was a shade over thirty years old when he became a star, and he had spent enough time inside the studio to know what he wanted. Born in rural Arkansas, Campbell moved west, playing beerjoints as he went. In 1960, he reached Los Angeles, and joined a fast-fading rock 'n' roll band, the Champs. He hung around Rick Nelson for a while, then became a session man, subbing occasionally for Brian Wilson in the Beach Boys. He said later that reaching for the Beach Boys'

high harmonies added an extra octave to his range. Driving to a session one day, he heard John Hartford's "Gentle on My Mind" on the radio. "The song had such a freshness of spirit," he wrote later. "It was an essay on life as I viewed it then." His hit version was a rehearsal in which he was demonstrating the song to other musicians, but it had the looseness and informality that the song demanded.

It was the partnership between Glen Campbell and Jimmy Webb that changed country music. Webb was from Elk City, Oklahoma, and moved with his family to southern California when he was eighteen. He pitched some songs to rock 'n' roll star Johnny Rivers, and "By the Time I Get to Phoenix" was among them. Rivers buried the song on an album, but Campbell heard it and immediately covered it.

Webb asked Campbell over to his house and played him "Wichita Lineman." Campbell liked it to the point of using the organ that Webb had played on the demo. It was an impressionistic piece: Webb had seen a lineman high atop a telephone pole out in the middle of nowhere, and had written a little meditation on what he might be thinking. In December 1968 it topped the country charts, and reached number three on the pop charts. Nothing as abstract had reached the country charts since Roy Acuff's "Great Speckle Bird." Hawaiian star Don Ho was the first to record Webb's "Galveston," but it became Campbell's masterpiece. Set in the Vietnam era, it was, as Webb later said, "about what it would be like to be a soldier far from home. My own departure seemed imminent. Galveston is not an east or west coast town. He's a kid from a small town. He's not afraid to admit he's afraid."

Campbell's success led to an invitation to host a television show, *The Glen Campbell Goodtime*

opposite Charley Pride: Guess who's coming to play *The Opry*?
above The intolerant side of country.

Hour, which first aired in May 1969, and became a top-rated series for three years. The writers included Steve Martin and Rob Reiner. With *The Johnny Cash Show* on ABC and *The Glen Campbell Goodtime Hour* on CBS, country music had finally arrived on prime time. Campbell and Cash, both raised in Depression-era Arkansas, were ideal poster boys for the changing face of country music. Campbell looked like a corn-fed every mother's son, but some of his hits addressed the era's problems, and many of them broadened the scope of country music.

It seemed as though country music was shedding its old skin, but that perception wasn't entirely valid. True, country music's first black superstar, Charley Pride, was charting record after record, and the Byrds made a token appearance on *The Grand Ole Opry*, but the hard, reactionary core of country fans was wondering what had happened to their world. They were mad and getting madder every time Jane Fonda appeared on television with her arm around the Vietcong or at the head of an anti-war march. The 1950s' country star Faron Young had an on-stage rap during the mid-to-late 1960s in which he would castigate the draft-card burners. "They ain't Americans. They're just some idiots we allow to live here," he would say. "You take the Beatles. Four guys who could have led America and the world's youth in a damned straight line. Instead, they caused dissent where it was unnecessary."

There had been political songs from the very dawn of recorded country music, but, in the polarized climate of the late 1960s, country music became the rallying cry of the far right. At the farthest extreme stood Reb Rebel Records, which didn't stand so much as hide behind a post-office box in Crowley, Louisana. The owner, J. D. Miller, was the sometime manager of Lefty Frizzell, writer of "It Wasn't God Who Made Honky Tonk Angels," and producer of many swamp blues artists, such as Slim Harpo and Lazy Lester. At their least odious, Reb Rebel records were fairly harmless jeremiads like "What Has Happened to Old Glory?" and "Dear Mr. President" ("My white coon dog won't hunt with my black coon dog/Can you take out an injunction to make them hunt together?") but the label's biggest seller was the hugely offensive "Johnny Rebel," who recorded songs such as "Move Them Niggers North," "Looking for a Handout," and "In Coon Town." Johnny Rebel was actually a Cajun singer named Cliff Trahan, who had cut some rockabilly singles in earlier times and recorded for Paul Cohen's Todd Records in the late 1950s. Apparently, he remained true to his credo, refusing to accept government social security checks after his retirement. His records were on open sale throughout the South in the late 1960s.

In 1970, the right-wing backlash finally reached the charts when Guy Drake had a top five country hit with "Welfare Cadillac," but if Marty Robbins had had his way, he would have been there four years earlier. In 1966, Robbins tried to release "Ain't I Right" and "My Own Native Land" as a single. He recorded for Columbia Records, and the label had just turned down Bob Dylan's "Talking John Birch Society Blues," so they were at least being even-handed in turning down Robbins' single. "Ain't I Right" was against the freedom riders coming into the South from points north.

The son of a Polish immigrant, Robbins was passionately anti-communist, anti-big government, and anti-foreign aid. His sideman, Bobby Sykes, takes up the story: "Columbia said, 'You can sue us, or do whatever you like, but this is not coming out on Columbia Records.' It was too political. Too explosive. So Marty took the same pickers, same singers, the Jordanaires, went back into the studio, cut it with me singing, and put it out as 'Johnny Freedom' on Sims Records. I heard it caused one station in Colorado Springs to be burned down. It was number one on some stations. It was too politically truthful."

The furor that greeted Merle Haggard's "Okie from Muskogee" is some indication of what would have happened if Robbins' record had appeared. Haggard, of course, welcomed the fight, much as Robbins would have. No one, with the possible exception of Loretta Lynn, so effectively mined their background for material as Merle Haggard. Jail, relationships that soured, mamas who tried, papas who died, the ever-beckoning swinging bar-room door. No one has ever made it any clearer where they've been or where they stand. His two stabs at

an autobiography fill in the remaining blanks. Whether singing his own songs or someone else's, Merle Haggard's music forms a tapestry in which the parts mesh seamlessly. If there's a recurring theme, it's his inability to fit. Anyone who has ever felt alone in a crowd or in a relationship, or anyone who would rather screw up than follow the manual finds an echo of themselves in Merle Haggard.

The story, in essence at least, is well known. Haggard was born in Bakersfield, California, to a family of Oklahoma migrants. His sister, though, is adamant that the family's move west was nothing like *The Grapes of Wrath*, and she should know because she was there and Merle wasn't. The

Haggards had been in Illinois until the cold set in, then they'd gone to California, back to Oklahoma, and then back again to California. A suspected arson attack on their barn, not the dust, finally sent them to California for good. Merle was born when his siblings were in their teens, so he essentially grew up an only child. The family lived in a boxcar when he was born, but it was temporary accommodation until a house they were building in Oildale was ready.

After his father's death, Haggard drifted into a cycle of petty crime that became increasingly less petty until he ended up at the gates of San Quentin on March 26, 1958. All told, he served two years

and nine months of a five-year sentence, then caught the bus back to Bakersfield to claw out a career in country music. Almost fifteen years to the day after he went inside, he was playing at the White House. Merle Haggard gravitated to country music because it was all about his life. He was a couple of years younger than Elvis, but rock 'n' roll didn't move him. The music Merle loved was the music that Nashville was leaving behind: Hank Williams, Bob Wills, Lefty Frizzell, and Jimmie Rodgers. "About the time I started to screw up, I'd learned to play pretty good guitar," he said. His brother had left a guitar and some records at home, and Merle figured out the chords. He was entering Bakersfield talent shows when his career took a hiatus.

In his first autobiography, *Sing Me Back Home*, Haggard talked about his career taking off in 1962. "It was like hoppin' a slow freight in the yard," he wrote, "and watching the people around you scramble to get on board too. You put out your hand to help them, but some just can't quite reach you. You know you could jump off and stay, but hell, you've tried so hard and so long to make the grab, you just can't let go. Besides, the wheels are turning faster and you're afraid that once you jump off this train, you might never catch another."

His sound was rooted in Bakersfield, not Nashville, and he cemented the connection by marrying Buck Owens' ex-wife, Bonnie. In early interviews, he was cagey about how he'd spent the two years and nine months he was inside. He had been an oil worker, he said, and hadn't played much because he was out in the bush. He added that he'd changed jobs often—a year here, a year there. Then Johnny Cash, who'd spent no more than a few nights in jail, made it chic to have a prison record, and Haggard came out with songs such as "Sing Me Back Home," "Branded Man," and "Mama Tried." Nashville beckoned, but Haggard politely declined. "When I began to gain popularity people started calling for me to come and play *The Grand Ole Opry*, asked me to become a member. This was in '67, but we didn't feel that we wanted to give up twenty-six Saturday nights a year and give up our place of origin, and move everything to Nashville. We said, 'Why would we want to go down there and get lost in the shuffle?' I'm very honored, but I really didn't know how to play Nashville music."

In the late 1960s, Merle Haggard gave a voice to those who might not buy Reb Rebel records, but nevertheless felt alienated within their own country.

His defiant blue-collar anthems, "Okie from Muskogee" and "Fightin' Side of Me," might have been half tongue in cheek, but they tapped into a well of resentment that few suspected was there. Merle Haggard, even more than Johnny Rebel, made it clear that protest was not the exclusive preserve of the hirsute, the left-leaning, and the young. Haggard's father once lived near Muskogee, and Haggard was on his tour bus when he saw a sign saying "Muskogee 19 Miles." A band member joked that they probably didn't smoke marijuana in Muskogee, and twenty minutes later Merle had the song written. "The Fightin' Side of Me" was even more unambiguous:

I read about some squirrely guy,
Who claims, he just don't believe in fightin'.
An' I wonder just how long,
The rest of us can count on bein' free.
They love our milk an' honey,
But they preach about some other way of livin'.
When they're runnin' down my country, hoss,
They're walkin' on the fightin' side of me.

Merle Haggard was on safer ground when he mined personal relationships. "I'm Always on a Mountain When I Fall" was chillingly autobiographical, despite the fact that Haggard didn't write it. "If We Make It Through December" was a Christmas song, but not one that Perry Como would have touched. "I Think I'll Just Stay Here and Drink" unambiguously related his ups and downs with the bottle. Haggard has never spared himself. Lately, he has ranted about radio's unwillingness to play older artists, but his *If Only I Could Fly* album, released in 2000, included a song titled "Wishing All These Old Things Were New." It began, "Watching while some old friends do a line/Holding back the want-to in my own addicted mind."

Chapter 15

HARD HAT DAYS
and Honky-tonk Nights

Merle Haggard was written up in *Rolling Stone* and loomed large in two late 1960s' books about country music (Paul Hemphill's *The Nashville Sound* and John Grissim's *Country Music: White Man's Blues*), but it was the success of Glen Campbell that seemed to point the way forward. In the early 1970s, record men came up with a new category: "middle of the road."

MoR, as it became known, was designed to reach those aged between twenty-five and forty, who had grown up on rock 'n' roll, but felt alienated by 1960s' and '70s' rock. Nashville enviously eyed MoR's market share and the number of stations that played MoR music. If a few more hillbilly edges were sanded down, country music could seize that profitable mid-ground, thus creating a new hybrid.

The era of MoR is indelibly associated with Olivia Newton-John. Born in England and raised in Australia, she became a lightning rod for all those who lamented what was happening to country music, despite the fact that she scored relatively few country hits and never claimed that she was "country." Rather than forsaking country for pop, she was heading in the opposite direction, and might have been no more than a footnote in country music history had she not won the Female Vocalist of the Year award at the 1974 Country Music Association (CMA) show. The award was the problem. It seemed as though country music had been hijacked, and Newton-John only stoked the resentment when she said she'd like to meet Hank Williams, who,

above Conway Twitty: rockabilly.
opposite Olivia Newton-John.

of course, had been dead for over twenty years. On November 4, 1974, right after the CMA awards, there was a midnight meeting at George Jones' and Tammy Wynette's house which resulted in the formation of the Association of Country Entertainers (ACE). The stated purpose was "to preserve the identity of country music as a separate and distinct form of entertainment." Ironically, the CMA had been formed as a rearguard action in 1958, when country music was under threat from rock 'n' roll, but now it seemed a little too willing to embrace pop crossover. The artists at George and Tammy's house that night included Brenda Lee, Bill Anderson, Barbara Mandrell, Billy Walker, Dolly Parton, Hank Snow, Conway Twitty, Porter Wagoner, and Faron Young, many of whom had cut rock 'n' roll and pop records in the past, and would again. Now, though, they were protesting against the dilution of their music, and against the fact that pop artists had hijacked country radio playlists. "Efforts to take country music to a wider audience will dilute it to the point that it no longer exists as an artform," declared Billy Walker. ACE was vocal but short-funded, and wound itself up in September 1981.

The artist who really embodied MoR country was Charlie Rich, but nobody begrudged him his success because they knew how long and how hard he'd worked for it. The world according to Charlie Rich was one in which Duke Ellington coexisted happily alongside Jimmy Reed, Frank Sinatra, Ray Charles, and Stan Kenton. Country didn't really figure into his thinking at all, and was perhaps the least likely place for him to make his mark. Rich grew up in rural Arkansas, and learned saxophone and piano. By the early 1950s, he was a polished performer—east Arkansas's answer to Mel Tormé. In 1957, his wife took one of his tapes to Sun Records in Memphis. Sun's musical director, Bill Justis, gave her some Jerry Lee Lewis records and told her to tell Charlie to come in when he'd gotten that bad. By 1958, Rich was on salary at Sun as a songwriter and session pianist, but Jerry Lee Lewis's career self-destructed, and Johnny Cash quit. Suddenly the two Sun artists capable of delivering a decent paycheck to a songwriter were gone or in disgrace. Against his will, Rich began recording for Sun, and his third single, "Lonely Weekends," became a top thirty hit in 1960. Rich made some brilliant, eccentric music at Sun. "Who Will the Next Fool Be?" is one of the era's most perfectly realized recordings, but it wasn't country.

After leaving Sun, Rich scored another big hit with "Mohair Sam," but was almost invisible by the time he signed with Columbia Records' Epic division in 1967. Epic's Nashville office was run by a former Sun engineer, Billy Sherrill, and for five years Charlie Rich was Sherrill's personal indulgence. Rich's records darted in and out of the charts, but anyone else as unsuccessful would have been dropped. His albums were eclectic: blues, pop standards, soul,

above Charlie Rich burns the card announcing that John Denver has won Entertainer of the Year, 1975.
opposite Conway Twitty.

and an occasional country song. Then, in 1972, Sherrill's marketing manager saw the opportunity in the new MoR market, and convinced Rich to concentrate his efforts on just one style for a change. Rich had no misgivings about deserting country because he had never been country. In April 1973, "Behind Closed Doors" topped the country charts, and reached the pop top twenty. "The Most Beautiful Girl" topped both charts. Hit followed hit.

Vegas beckoned, but Rich, who had been plagued by self-doubt and stage fright throughout his career, became troubled by what was happening. "It's great that you're booking the jobs," he said, "and making the money and pleasing the folks, but it's awful hard if you entered the thing creatively in the first place. It's awful hard to create songs and get new ideas...if you have to play the same show that's popular, and you have to play primarily the songs people know." He seesawed precariously between wanting all that his career now seemed to promise, and wanting to go back to the familiar

supper clubs and bar-rooms where he could pick up a small band and structure his set as he wanted. A haunting demo of "Feel Like Going Home" captured the disillusionment, but of course it wasn't released at the time.

At the 1975 CMA awards, Charlie Rich set fire to the envelope announcing that John Denver had won the Entertainer of the Year award. Was it an unconscious act of musical criticism or a veiled request to get out? By 1980, the hits had slowed to a trickle, and Rich retreated behind the wrought-iron gates of his five-acre estate in the Germantown suburb of Memphis. At the height of his success, there was talk of a briefcase full of unpublished songs that he would perform once he felt confident moving from country into something else. That briefcase, if it ever existed, was almost a metaphor for the career that he never had. It was indicative of his ambivalence toward country music that he never moved to Nashville; the east end of Memphis was as close as he got.

Rich embodied another minor trend: rockabillies returning to country music. Two other former Sun artists, Conway Twitty and Jerry Lee Lewis, led the charge. Twitty's statistics were astonishing. He was the best-charting country star of the 1970s, ran a close second in the 1980s, and scored more number one country hits than anyone else. His rock 'n' roll career held one luminous moment, "It's Only Make Believe," but when the music changed in the mid-1960s, he realized that his fans weren't listening anymore, so he changed direction. Despite what he said later, he didn't quit at the top of his game, but just switching represented a giant leap of faith. In the spring of 1965, he walked out halfway through a show at a kids' vacation spot, hired a steel guitarist, and began booking himself as a country singer at $200 a night. No one even imagined such a transition was possible. In the years ahead, rockabillies would forsake rock 'n' roll in droves, declaring that they had always been country, but Twitty was first. His vision of country music was defiantly hardcore.

While some were taking the music uptown, Twitty held fast to his blue-collar look: pompadour, sideburns, sportshirt, no hair over the ears, no Nehru jacket. And he had a blue-collar sound to match. The tempo rarely strayed above medium-fast, and he took full advantage of his range, setting the stage with sotto voce introductions, building slowly on the bridge, and closing with high drama. It was an approach that worked especially well on his "bedroom ballads." Astutely judged to stay just inside the line, they said what men supposedly wanted to say—but couldn't, and what women wanted to hear—but didn't. And just as Twitty's rock 'n' roll career had a defining moment, so did his country career. "Hello Darlin'" begins with very short spoken intro, establishing the regret that

permeates the record. It's the only time the title is mentioned in the song, thus confounding every rule of country songwriting. The song then takes the form of a conversation heard from one side, and Twitty never once lets the tension slip. It's a great performance, taut and economical. At that point in Twitty's career, it mirrored a generation stumbling into adulthood. Whether rockin' on *Bandstand* or crooning in Branson, Twitty knew his crowd.

Conway Twitty didn't try to reach pop radio after his 1965 conversion, but that wasn't true of country music in general. Its next best shot at reaching a broader audience came in the post-disco void of 1980. Throughout the late 1970s, disco's techno beats were omnipresent, and some stations even changed format to all-disco. The catalyst was a 1977 movie, *Saturday Night Fever*, starring John Travolta. The movie mass-marketed New York's underground club world, and made Travolta into a star. But the disco craze ended as quickly as it had begun, and it ended, as most crazes end, with trucks lined up at record company receiving bays with cartons of returns. Ironically, it was Travolta who prompted the next craze with his appearance in *Urban Cowboy*. Yet another subculture was mass-marketed and trivialized.

In the summer of 1978, Rice University's Continuing Studies program invited *Esquire* magazine editor Clay Felker to speak, and after his talk, two members of the program took him to Gilley's in the Houston oil refinery suburb of Pasadena. Gilley's had opened in 1971 as a joint venture between Jerry Lee Lewis's cousin, Mickey Gilley, and his manager, Sherwood Cryer. It was open more or less all day (its slogan was "We doze but we never close"). Topping out at 48,000 square feet, it was the world's largest honky-tonk. Felker was fascinated by the rootless and restless lives of the oil workers, and commissioned an article by Aaron Latham ("The Ballad of the Urban Cowboy"), which appeared in September 1978. The article's centerpiece was an unusual love triangle: a man, a woman, and Gilley's mechanical bull. Latham's big idea was that when America searches for direction, the cowboy comes to the rescue, but this time the cowboy was riding a mechanical bull, and not doing it as well as his girl-friend. Latham was immediately contacted about movie rights, and *Urban Cowboy* became an iconic motion picture, albeit one that hasn't weathered the years too well.

"Hard-hat days and honky-tonk nights" was the slogan. Gilley's became an unlikely national shrine, and little Gilley's opened in such unlikely places as New York and Washington. Disco outfits were suddenly exchanged for western duds. The *Urban Cowboy* movie soundtrack album topped the pop LP charts and made Gilley into a star. Johnny Lee's "Lookin' for Love" not only captured the feel of the movie, but became the song that ruled the summer of 1980.

Urban Cowboy came at a time when radio was changing once more. The new format was called Adult Contemporary, or AC for short, and the idea on Nashville's Music Row was that country music could colonize this new hybrid. AC's basic premise was, as *Time* magazine put it, "not [to play] what the listeners actually like, but what they find least offensive." In 1981, it looked very much as though Music Row's dreams were coming true. Country music sales doubled that year, reaching $500 million, or roughly 15 percent of all record retail sales. The Nashville labels began cultivating a new breed of country star. Janie Fricke, Sylvia, Earl Thomas Conley, Ronnie Milsap, and T. G. Sheppard could cross into AC. But then, as with disco, the boom ended, and the trucks lined up at the receiving bays bearing

returns. By 1983, country music sales were back at pre-1981 levels. Gilley's closed in New York and Washington, but the Texas hub remained open until 1989. In January 1985, *Variety* magazine ran a headline, "Country Music Sales Turn Sour." It was time to look inward for country music's uniqueness rather than outward in search of something pop radio might like.

Chapter 16

NASHVILLE
Rebels

It was part marketing and part flimflammery, but at least partly genuine. The genuine part was probably Texas cussedness that never really wanted to do things the Nashville way. After a couple of years, "outlaws" really meant nothing, but for a while it did, and when the smoke cleared, things would never again be quite the same in Nashville.

Unlike Steve Sholes, Don Law, Paul Cohen, and Ken Nelson, the new Nashville division heads lived in the city. They usually doubled as producers and had several other producers on call when the workload became too heavy. The label chiefs would have favorite session men and arrangers, and they'd have favorite music publishers—in fact, they'd often own their favorite music publisher. The artist was a small cog in all this. He or she would have some say in song choice, but usually could choose only between songs that the producer had preselected. The label essentially called the shots.

"The Outlaws" turned the artist/label paradigm on its head. The artist called the shots and the label would become the manufacturer and distributor of what the artist delivered. This, of course, was no innovation: creative control had been ceded to rock artists in the mid-1960s, and Elvis's manager, Colonel Parker, had battled RCA's Steve Sholes for the right to control song choice as far back as 1956. By the time Elvis left the army in 1960, the Colonel exercised complete control. The Colonel's concern, of course, was not artistic; he wanted Elvis to sing songs controlled by their publishing partnerships, and the outcome

above Waylon Jennings playing the Nashville game.
opposite Willie Nelson playing it too.

was disastrous. By 1967, Elvis was recording songs that he owned to the virtual exclusion of all others, but no one was buying them. Around the same time, there were bins full of unsold, hugely self-indulgent rock albums that desperately needed a real producer. Artistic control wasn't everything it was cracked up to be, but it was what Waylon Jennings and Willie Nelson wanted. Both of them had been recording since the late 1950s, and after fifteen years in the system, they'd decided that if they couldn't make music their way, they'd just go home.

Waylon Jennings was born about forty miles northwest of Buddy Holly's birthplace in Lubbock, and Holly's success lit a fire under him. "Everything in music," Holly told Waylon, "falls in place from the rhythm." Waylon would later rediscover that truth when he began producing himself. In 1958, he was a dee-jay on KLLL in Lubbock, and Holly was hanging out at the station. That September they went to Norman Petty's studio in Clovis, New

Mexico, and Waylon cut a garbled version of "Jole Blon" with Holly in the producer's chair. Holly needed money, so he went out on the road across the coldest part of the country in the middle of winter, and he asked Waylon to join him as his bass player. On January 23, 1959, Waylon got a leave of absence from KLLL, and flew to Chicago to join the tour. It ended, of course, ten days later in a frozen Iowa cornfield. Waylon was supposed to have ridden in the plane that took Buddy's life, but gave up his seat to the Big Bopper. For the next thirty-five years, he would refuse to fly on February 3.

"I went a little nuts," Waylon said later. "I wouldn't play or nothin', and I was probably feeling sorry for myself that my whole world had blown up. I've never been that much of a man with religious faith, so I just didn't understand it from that angle. And I just couldn't see the sense of it from another angle, and I felt guilty. I was quittin' one job, and going over here for a hundred dollars a month more. I was a good disc-jockey. I was pretty funny, and a little ahead of my time... I had to do something to stay in music. Subconsciously I always knew I'd be back to it, but consciously I was hollerin' that I didn't want nothin' else to do with it."

He went to Coolidge, Arizona, back to Texas, and then, in 1960, on to Phoenix. He became a local legend in Phoenix, and began recording folk-rock music for A&M. People began to take notice. Willie Nelson passed through and told him *not* to go to Nashville, but Bobby Bare told him that he should be in Nashville and on RCA Records. Bare applied pressure on Chet Atkins at RCA, and, as of March 1965, Waylon was on RCA, and, as of April 1966, he was a resident of Nashville. He tried hard to fit in,

but chafed under the restrictions. For every great record, such as "Only Daddy Who'll Walk the Line," there were many mediocre ones. It was hard to say no to Chet Atkins because Atkins was an honorable and decent man, and demanded awe from anyone who aspired to play the guitar, as Waylon did. But then Atkins gave the task of producing Waylon Jennings to an arranger, Danny Davis, who led a band called the Nashville Brass. Waylon finally blew up, waving a pistol around in the studio, infuriated that Davis was overdubbing his tracks without his assent. He hired Miles Davis's manager, Neil Reshen, to renegotiate his contract, and in December 1972 he recorded *Lonesome, On'ry and Mean* with his road band and with himself as producer. And thus the outlaw movement began.

Waylon had heard fellow Texan Billy Joe Shaver sing backstage at a Texas music festival, and Bobby Bare later introduced them, but Shaver had to force his way into a session before Waylon really listened to his songs. "[They] were all of a piece," Waylon wrote in his autobiography, "and the only way you could understand Billy Joe was to hear his whole body of work." The result was Waylon's *Honky Tonk Heroes*, a landmark album. It had rock 'n' roll attitude and a rock 'n' roll mix. Ralph Mooney's steel guitar threaded through it, but the prevailing sound was guitar, bass, and drums. The album was produced by Tompall Glaser, who, like Waylon and Willie, had kicked around the industry since the late 1950s. "You just can't believe how different everything sounded when he moved from RCA over to my studio," said Tompall. "The bottom [end of the sound] was fat and big again and like it was on the road. You could hear the drum, it went with a little kick in the back. Marvellous. His band were all professional musicians but couldn't get the time of day in studios in Nashville because they weren't part of the A or B team, so we used them and you could feel the energy in the music. It had an edge." The albums that followed – *Ramblin' Man*, *This Time*, *Dreamin' My Dreams* – were equally good. To that

point, the format of Nashville albums had been "one hit plus nine filler tracks." Now Waylon, like Cash before him, began recording albums as integrated works, inviting the label to find the single.

The Nashville system could still deliver a surprise, though. Owen Bradley's son, Jerry, had taken over RCA's Nashville division in 1973 after Chet Atkins' resignation. (Owen, meanwhile, was still head of Decca/MCA's country division.) Bradley saw that Willie Nelson was successful on Columbia and that Waylon's wife, Jessi Colter, was successful on Capitol, and he knew that RCA owned back catalog on both artists. Under the terms of Waylon's new

contract, they couldn't pull tracks from the new albums, but they could compile from the old work, so Bradley assembled an album from the back catalog that he called *Wanted: The Outlaws*. Tompall Glaser's publicist, Hazel Smith, had dubbed Waylon, Willie, Billy Joe Shaver, and Glaser "the outlaws" from Waylon's *Ladies Love Outlaws* LP, and it stuck. Bradley didn't want Glaser on the album because he owned none of his catalog, but Waylon insisted on it. Glaser wouldn't sign the contracts, so Bradley called him: "'Tompall this is Bradley. I got two sets of artwork here, one with your picture on it, and one without your picture on it and if you don't get that damned contract over here in fifteen minutes, I'm sending the one without it to New York.' About fifteen minutes later, knock-knock-knock. It's Tompall. To be honest, I thought it would probably sell 500–600,000, but it was the first country record to go a million. Back in the '70s that had a tremendous impact."

Wanted: The Outlaws bracketed Waylon Jennings with Willie Nelson in the public mind, but for all they had in common, they came from different directions and would ultimately go their separate ways. Waylon's background was rockabilly and hillbilly; Willie's was western swing, jazz, folk, and pop. Willie Nelson arrived in Nashville in 1960 and stayed eleven years. He came for the reasons they still come: to write songs and make records. He knew he had the goods because one of his songs, "Family Bible," was a fair-sized hit in 1960, although the only money he'd seen for it was the $50 he'd received when he sold it. At least it proved that he could write a hit. Mae Axton, once Colonel Parker's PR person and the cowriter of "Heartbreak Hotel," had met Willie in Vancouver, Washington, where he was working as a dee-jay. She'd told him to go back to Texas or on to Nashville. Nelson had gone to Vancouver in 1956, and cut his first single there in 1957 for his own Willie Nelson Records, but rather than go to Nashville, he went first to the Houston suburb of Pasadena. George Jones's manager/producer, Pappy Daily, was in Houston, and Nelson cut two singles for Daily's "D" Records. The first appeared in July 1959. A local musician bought "Family Bible" from Willie, and placed it with Claude Gray, who recorded it for "D" in December 1959. As it started to break, Nelson got the urge to

opposite Twilight of the gods—Willie Nelson and Merle Haggard.
above Willie Nelson, hog farmer.

move on. Just before he left, he wrote "Night Life." Daily wouldn't release it on "D", so Nelson recorded it pseudonymously for the tiny Rx label.

Early in 1960, Willie dropped off his wife and kids with his in-laws and headed for Nashville. "That was where the store was," he wrote in his autobiography. "If I had anything to sell, it must be taken to the store." He moved into a trailer park where Roger Miller had lived a few years earlier. Hank Cochran, writer of Patsy Cline's "I Fall to Pieces," signed him to Ray Price's Pamper Music. Price took "Night Life" and Faron Young took "Hello Walls." The session musicians thought "Hello Walls" was an especially stupid song. "They'd walk around and say, 'Hello guitar,' 'Hello microphone,'" said Young, "and I said, 'That's good, laugh, 'cause it's gonna be a hit.' My first check was like $22,000. Willie had only collected maybe $1500 or $1800 as a writer. He came to me and said he needed $1500, and he offered to sell me 'Hello Walls' for $1500. I said, 'Willie, don't sell that song, it's already done 600,000 records,' but he thought I was hyping him. I said, 'How much money do you really need?' He said, 'Five hundred dollars,' and I gave him five hundred and made him swear to me that he would not sell that song. Another six or seven weeks went by and Willie's next check was something like

$14,000. I was sitting in Tootsie's Orchid Lounge having a beer when suddenly this big arm came around my neck, pulled me and pinched my jaw, and Willie Nelson French-kissed me. I ain't never been kissed that good in my life."

Then Patsy Cline recorded "Crazy" and Billy Walker cut the first version of "Funny (How Time Slips Away)." On the strength of his songwriting success, Willie was signed to Liberty Records and dented the charts for the first time as a performer. Liberty let him go, and Willie used his royalties to buy a hog farm near Nashville. Then, in 1964, Chet Atkins signed him to RCA. Roger Miller was selling millions of records for Mercury, and Atkins (who'd had Miller under contract and let him go), probably saw Willie Nelson filling the void. Nelson spent nine years on RCA, as Atkins and others tried to find a bridge between his quirky style and something country radio would play. Only in Texas, where his audience was steadily growing, could he fill a hall. Texans saw him carrying on the tradition of Bob Wills, Ernest Tubb, and crazy old Floyd Tillman. Things began falling apart around 1969. The farm burned down and he had a child with a woman in Texas to the surprise of his second wife in Nashville. He moved to the Happy Valley Dude Ranch in Bandera, Texas, then on to Austin. His last RCA album, *Yesterday's Wine*, was conceptual, sparsely produced, and featured spoken segues. It was very close to the style with which he would find success, but it sold so poorly that RCA dropped him.

The next time Willie Nelson recorded, it was for Atlantic Records, then in the process of launching a country division. Two Willie Nelson albums later, Atlantic wound up its Nashville office. Tompall Glaser says he tried to persuade Atlantic to keep Willie on the roster. "I went to see [Atlantic president] Ahmet Ertegun to talk to him about

keeping Nashville open and he called in one of his assistants. 'What do you think of Willie Nelson?' The guy laughs. Willie went on to sell 40 million records! They could have kept him." Nelson went back to Texas to record *Red Headed Stranger* for $12,000 in a jingle studio. He had been signed by Columbia Records' New York office, but New York assigned him to Billy Sherrill in Nashville. Sherrill produced Charlie Rich and Tammy Wynette, and didn't understand anything about *Red Headed Stranger*. New York had to insist upon its release. It wasn't radically different from the last RCA album or the two Atlantic albums, but where those had sold in the low thousands, *Red Headed Stranger* sold millions. Columbia pulled Fred Rose's 1945 song "Blue Eyes Crying in the Rain" as the single from the album, and it became a number one hit.

If Waylon's touchstone was Buddy Holly, Willie Nelson seemed to reach back to an imaginary point where Floyd Tillman bisected with Django Reinhardt. His *Stardust* album of pop oldies was another unlikely concept that sold millions. He made and lost a fortune. "No, let's not plan," he told his accountant, shortly after the IRS had nailed him for $9 million in back taxes, "it's more fun if you don't." Nelson's July 4 picnics in Dripping Springs, Texas, made him a Lone Star legend, and helped make nearby Austin into the USA's alternative country music capital. Folk singers such as Jerry Jeff Walker congregated there alongside psychedelic era cast-offs such as the Thirteenth Floor Elevators and Doug Sahm. "Austin has always been a performing place," said Nelson. "They still have probably per capita more performing places than any other place. Nashville was just the opposite; it was publishing companies and recording companies and there weren't that many places to play." Willie Nelson became iconic in a way that Waylon Jennings never did. He epitomized more than music. Like Jimmy Buffett, he suggested a lifestyle. He brought together different constituencies: rednecks, hippies, and blue-collar workers. He has recorded so prolifically that a complete Willie Nelson collection is an impossibility. Along the way, he has saluted his heroes, such as Floyd Tillman and Lefty Frizzell, and seemingly recorded duets with anyone who asked him. He has been the ultimate rule-breaker. "I think fearlessness and stupidity go together," he says.

The success of Waylon Jennings and Willie Nelson inevitably focused attention on others within their orbit. Studio owner and recording artist Tompall Glaser had been an outsider, if not an outlaw, all his life. A Jewish kid growing up on a farm in Nebraska listening to Ernest Tubb, he was born to non-conform. He sang with gruff, self-mocking insolence, and knocked around Nashville for forty-five years, rubbing shoulders with the very successful, but never quite joining them. With his brothers Chuck and Jim, he joined Marty Robbins' package show in Nebraska and began recording for Robbins' shortlived record label. They subbed for the Jordanaires in the studio, worked on the road with Johnny Cash, and tried different styles. Their first major success was as music publishers when they acquired John Hartford's "Gentle on My Mind." The Glasers' records darted in and out of the charts, and they split in 1973. Tompall took over their studio. Dubbed Hillbilly Central, it was open all hours. "When we started," he said, "people thought we were going to destroy Nashville. Who wants to destroy Nashville? If you've got a good, decent alternative, all you've got to do is keep doing it, and pretty soon the whole industry will be doing it." And pretty soon, they were.

One of the first to jump on the outlaw bandwagon was David Allan Coe, but his music soon became inextricably entangled with his self-created myth. Did he really kill a man in jail? Was he really a polygamist? Did he really drop his pants at Nashville's Exit/In? Did he make those X-rated albums to sell to bikers? The truths, half-truths, and lies got him noticed, but the sideshows hid the music. Coe was from Akron, Ohio, and served plenty of time throughout his youth. His fellow inmates included Charles Manson and Screamin' Jay Hawkins. In 1968, he arrived in Nashville and began recording and songwriting. His first major hit as a songwriter

was Tanya Tucker's "Would You Lay with Me in a Field of Stone?" A few years later, producer Billy Sherrill gave Coe's classic blue-collar anthem "Take This Job and Shove It," to another artist, Johnny Paycheck. As a result, Coe's tally is thirty or so

mostly forgettable minor hits. "If I had it to do over," he says, "Nashville would have never seen David Allan Coe. I was suppressed here in Nashville. Waylon and Willie got real famous. I felt like Bob Dylan in those early days. He was the guy in the background responsible for all these things that were happening, and writing songs that other people were having hits with, but he wasn't getting the recognition. Then, all of a sudden, people found out who he was, and I thought the same thing would happen to me. The paths all led to David Allan Coe, but it never did happen."

Hank Williams, Jr. was the outlaw with a private income. For all the hits, now numbering around 100, perhaps his greatest achievement was escaping his father's long shadow. While the offspring of other country stars, such as Marty Robbins, Conway Twitty, and Buck Owens, were unable to sustain music careers, "Junior," as he's known, went from strength to strength. His mother, Audrey, planned his career as a tribute to his father, thereby stoking the legend upon which her livelihood depended. Signed to his father's record label, MGM, Junior's first public appearance as a recording artist was in Canton, Ohio, where his father would have performed had he not died en route. Junior toured with his father's band members, sang his father's songs for his father's label, added music to some lyrics his father had left, recorded some faked-up father-son duets, and even recorded narrations such as "Luke the Drifter, Jr." As an act of fealty, it worked; as music for the late 1960s, it did not. Turnout at the shows was good; record sales were generally poor. "At first," Junior told interviewer John Eskow, "I thought it was the greatest thing in the world—a ghost of this man that everyone loved. They think I'm Daddy. Mother's smilin', money's rolling in, seemed ideal." By 1970, it seemed less so, and Junior's distress only mounted as MGM edged him away from the tribute act toward country-pop. His first number one hit, "All for the Love of Sunshine," was every bit as vacuous as it sounded.

The outlaw movement began coalescing around Waylon Jennings and Willie Nelson, and its anti-Nashville stance and rock 'n' roll attitude appealed to Junior, but before long he discovered an even closer kinship with Southern rock bands such as Lynyrd Skynyrd and the Marshall Tucker Band. He wrestled himself free of his mother and Nashville. His music became swaggering, unapologetically sexist, hugely self-referential—and very successful. Of his thirty hits during the 1980s, seven peaked at number one. "All My Rowdy Friends Are Coming Over Tonight" was adopted as the theme of ABC-TV's top-rated *Monday Night Football*. Junior's musicality (he can play many instruments very well) came to the fore on a chart-topping revival of Fats Waller's "Ain't Misbehavin'" and on occasional album cuts, but it was the defiant bubbaness of songs such as "Good Friends, Good Whiskey, Good Lovin'," or "Naked Women and Beer" (his recent duet with rap rocker Kid Rock) that his audience seemed to want. Sensitive new age men may recoil, but as Junior himself says, "Hey, we don't all live in New York or Los Angeles."

The term "outlaws" soon became meaningless. At their peak, the outlaws were outselling everyone else in Nashville, and were thus mainstream. Anyone who double-parked on Music Row began calling themselves an outlaw. In 1978, Waylon Jennings recognized as much when he recorded "Don't You Think This Outlaw Bit's Done Got Out of Hand?" Jennings had passed his creative peak; Willie Nelson's seemingly bottomless well of songs had almost run dry; David Allan Coe's posturing had become tiresome; and Hank , Jr. was an honorary Allman Brother. Once again, it was time to move on.

opposite Hank Williams, Jr.
inset Hank, Jr, country youngster, with Faron Young.

Chapter 17

OLD WINE
in New Bottles

The outlaws' roots weren't altogether country. Waylon Jennings remained under the influence of Buddy Holly, while Willie Nelson loved an eclectic musical mix, only some of which was country. The outlaws looked like rock musicians, acted like rock musicians, and acquired the habits of rock musicians.

The next time country music tried going forward by going back, the reference points would be hillbilly, bluegrass, western swing, and honky-tonk.

As the outlaws faded from view, Nashville tried once more to find the land where pop and country meet. Alabama scored an unbroken string of twenty-one consecutive number one country singles between 1980 and 1987, and Ronnie Milsap scored an almost unbroken string of number one country singles between 1974 and 1989. Kenny Rogers, although not quite as popular as he'd been in the late 1970s, was still hugely successful in the early 1980s. And the Bellamy Brothers, a former soft rock band who'd written Jim Stafford's 1974 hit "Spiders and Snakes" before breaking through with "Let Your Love Flow" in 1976, moved very successfully into country music with some weakly punning songs—"If I Said You Had a Beautiful Body Would You Hold It Against Me," "Get into Reggae Cowboy," "Rebels without a Clue." The back-to-the-roots movement began in response to this diluted country pop and country rock. It had no clear starting point, but gathered momentum throughout the 1980s.

Emmylou Harris is a prophet with honor. Born in Birmingham, Alabama, she was the daughter of a career military man, and grew up in the Washington,

above George Strait.
opposite Emmylou Harris.

D.C. suburbs. She eventually won Nashville's respect for her touching faith in the music and for her ability to sell hundreds of thousands of albums, but didn't move there until 1983. The turning point in her career came twelve years earlier when she met the original cosmic cowboy, Gram Parsons, who was looking for a duet partner. To that point, Harris had been a folk singer with one not-very-good album behind her. "Gram," she says, "provided me with a way to connect, or reconnect, with something that was dormant but was definitely there." That "something" was country music. Later, Parsons told a friend that she was his "kick in the ass." Their crowd was cowboy hippies. "He did stone country stuff," she says. "He was serious about instructing

his audiences in country music, but he'd also have a rock 'n' roll medley because he knew that people need to cry but they also need to dance." But then, in September 1973, before their second Warner-Reprise album, *Return of the Grievous Angel*, was released, Parsons died in the California desert from too much tequila and grievous angel dust.

Warner Bros. Records kept Emmylou Harris on the roster, pairing her with Anne Murray's producer, Brian Ahern, whom she later married. She went into debt to assemble the best band she could afford: at one time or another it included James Burton, Albert Lee, Ricky Skaggs, and Rodney Crowell. Every year there was an album; some years there were two. Emmylou Harris became a postmodern songcatcher. Just as the first generation of songcatchers had gone to Appalachia in the early part of the twentieth century in search of the ancient ballads, so Emmylou Harris listened to cassettes people made for her and sought out unheralded songwriters. Perhaps no one has ever cared as deeply about every song on every album. "I believe that every song should have the emotional impact that'll make you want to pull your car off the highway and listen," she says. "There are too many songs that caricature life and feelings." Almost every album included at least one or two songs that make a statement about country music's roots. She recorded a bluegrass album, *Roses in the Snow*, at a time when bluegrass was marginalized to festivals and tiny labels. If Warner Bros. was surprised when the tape arrived, the surprise must have been compounded when *Roses in the Snow* became the fastest of her albums to earn a gold record. It was released in April 1980 and was certified gold (i.e. audited sales of 500,000) on April 1, 1981, and it achieved those sales without a major hit single and during the general market downturn of the early 1980s. Its success should have alerted the major labels to the potential of bluegrass music, but it didn't.

Roses in the Snow was made under the influence of Ricky Skaggs, who had replaced Rodney Crowell in Harris's Hot Band. In 1981, Skaggs left the Hot Band to begin a solo career. Although he was only twenty-seven, he had already been performing professionally for fifteen years. Born in Cordell, Kentucky, in 1954, he was invited onstage in 1959 to play mandolin alongside Bill Monroe. Ten years later, he formed a duet with Keith Whitley, and their setpiece was note-perfect imitations of the Stanley Brothers. The following year, they went to see Ralph Stanley in West

Virginia, but he was late, and the club owner asked them to go onstage. "I walked in," Ralph said later, "and these two boys were singing the Stanley Brothers' music better than the Stanley Brothers." He hired them both in 1971. Skaggs stayed until 1974, then played with various bluegrass and newgrass bands until joining Harris in 1977. His first solo album for Epic/Columbia Records, *Waitin' for the Sun to Shine*, appeared in 1981, fusing bluegrass and hardcore country. He later took the Stanley Brothers' "Don't Cheat in Our Hometown" and Bill Monroe's "Uncle Pen" to the top of the country charts (a feat that the Stanleys and Monroe had been unable to perform). Skaggs' career cooled in the late 1980s, and in 1997 he decided to stand or fall with bluegrass. He formed his own label, Skaggs Family Records, and in 2000 launched a companion roots label, Ceili Music, featuring Americana and Celtic music.

John Anderson kept a very different kind of traditional music alive during the early 1980s. His vocal style was rooted in Lefty Frizzell's quirky phrasing and note-bends, and his music sounded as if he'd grown up above an Alabama honky-tonk, although he was actually from Florida. Anderson arrived in Nashville in 1971 and worked on the construction of the new *Grand Ole Opry* house while trying to place his songs. Warner Bros. Records signed him in 1977 and kept the faith through some lean years. The turnaround came in 1981, when his recording of Billy Joe Shaver's "I'm Just an Old Chunk of Coal (But I'm Gonna Be a Diamond Someday)" reached number four. In 1983 his single "Swingin'" (pronounced "swangin'") topped the country charts and became the CMA single of the year. Despite the fact that he was surrounded by

opposite Ricky Skaggs with Emmylou Harris.

Kenny Rogers, Alabama, the Bellamy Brothers, and the Oak Ridge Boys, Anderson kept his music defiantly hardcore. His 1982 album *Wild and Blue* was honky-tonk nouveau at its finest. The songs were adult and the production by Don Law's former assistant Frank Jones was spare and hardhitting. Another Lefty Frizzell disciple, Merle Haggard, joined Anderson on Frizzell's "Long Black Veil." The album was the last to be recorded in Columbia's old Studio B, where Ray Price, Johnny Cash, Stonewall Jackson, Marty Robbins, and others had recorded so many classics, and it appeared in the year that Don Law finally drank himself to death in Texas. Ironically, the new traditionalist revival that Anderson had done much to pioneer, derailed his career in the late 1980s, but his records made an uncompromising statement about what was country at a time when the message was in danger of being lost.

If Ricky Skaggs' and Emmylou Harris's touchstone was bluegrass, and if John Anderson's was honky-tonk, then George Strait's major influence was western swing. Strait, born near San Antonio, Texas, was a couple of years older than Skaggs and Anderson, but still too young to remember western swing's heyday. His early listening was mostly confined to British Invasion rock bands, but during a stint in the army in the early 1970s, he discovered Merle Haggard's homage to Bob Wills, *Tribute to the Best Damn Fiddle Player in the World*, and began exploring country music. Returning home, he launched a band. George Jones' former manager, Pappy Daily, still ran his "D" label, and his son played in Strait's band. Strait's first single appeared on "D" in 1976, and he began to draw such huge crowds in east Texas that the major labels were forced to take notice. He tried a wide variety of material, but the core of it remained faithful to his western swing and honky-tonk roots. "I want to reach a point where people hear my name and immediately think of real country music," he said after signing with MCA in 1981, and he has certainly achieved that. He looked like an *Urban Cowboy* walk-on—starched white shirt, neatly pressed blue jeans, and Resistol cowboy hat—but

above John Anderson.
opposite Randy Travis.

Strait really was a rancher, and that was how he dressed. His first MCA single, "Unwound," reached number six in 1981, and every subsequent single reached the charts, long after singles themselves ceased to exist. He took songs from Lefty Frizzell's writer Whitey Shafer, and from Pappy Daily's former writer Royce Porter. Strait sounded mature, confident, and very much at ease with himself and his music. He rarely wrote his own material, but his music sounded like *his* music, rather than some confection that had been forced upon him. Through it all, Strait has remained remarkably centered. He stays in Texas and has remained married to his childhood sweetheart, venturing to Nashville only to make records. As soon as he could, he stopped doing interviews and cut back on his touring schedule to spend more time at his ranch. He gave 1990s' "new country" its look—and "look" suddenly became very important.

The year 1986 marked neo-traditionalism's new dawn. Randy Travis, Dwight Yoakam, Steve Earle, and Lyle Lovett had almost nothing in common except the year of their breakthrough, but that was enough for them to be bracketed together. Randy Travis's warm, understated baritone is one of country music's great voices, and his lantern-jawed good looks made him one of the first stars of Country Music Television (CMT). Launched as CMTV in 1983, CMT was a video cable channel designed to do for country music what MTV had done for rock. If it accomplished nothing else, it made record companies hyper-aware of how potential artists looked. Earlier generations of country stars had included some who were ungainly or obese. That would never happen again. Randy Travis sounded the part and looked the part. He absorbed the country music greats through his father's record

collection. Several convictions for petty crime seemed likely to derail his career (even when driving a stolen car, he later remembered, he always played a country station on the car radio), but a local nightspot owner, Lib Hatcher, began guiding his life and work. They moved to Nashville in 1981, but several years passed before Warner Bros. Records saw Travis's potential. The first single, "On the Other Hand," did poorly in 1985, but the follow-up, "1982," reached number six early in 1986. "On the Other Hand" was re-released and topped the charts. Travis's first album, *Storms of Life*, was uncompromising hard country, and surprised many within the industry by reaching number one on the country LP charts and selling 3 million copies. If *Storms of Life* had shown that Travis had a good ear for the forlorn, its follow-up, *Always and Forever*, showed that he had an equally good ear for the romantic. And the romantic won out; it stayed at the top of the country charts for forty-three weeks.

Travis was somewhat eclipsed when a new generation of even more telegenic stars appeared on the scene. He continued to record after Warners dropped him, he has appeared in movies, and he has toured, but he has never recaptured the moment in 1986 when hard country was resurgent and he was its poster boy.

Randy Travis was widely respected for the quietly assertive way he brought about an acknowledgment of the music's roots and for his vocal skills. Dwight Yoakam, on the other hand, was not only widely despised in Nashville, but didn't care. His spiky, brooding songs and his explicit debt to Bakersfield weren't the problem; it was his mouthiness. Never short of opinions, he reveled in having a soapbox at last. He castigated Nashville for its betrayal of country music; he castigated Columbia Records for dropping Johnny Cash. If you

had a subject, Dwight Yoakam had an opinion. He learned to be less abrasive, but "I don't recall…" will never be part of his vocabulary. His affinity for hillbilly music was come by honestly. Like Randy Travis, he grew up listening to his family's record collection. "There was just enough stuff there to educate me musically in an offbeat fashion," he says. "It was a non-radio programmed education. And even though we moved out of rural Kentucky when I was a kid, we'd go back to my grandparents' house and I'd hear the Louvin Brothers, Bill Monroe, and so on. In the late '60s, you could still hear unadulterated country music on the radio in the South—even live radio in Kentucky." Yoakam is proud of his Southern blue-collar background to the point of inverted snobbery, but the precariousness of those years has colored his approach to life. "There was always a question about whether we would be able to maintain our level of existence. It's given me an uneasiness about security—and the world. You hear that in country music. The cultural ethnicity of country music is the *Grapes of Wrath* culture."

Yoakam went to Nashville, then on to Los Angeles. He started playing the hillbilly nightspots, and in 1980 he met guitarist Pete Anderson at a club in the San Fernando Valley. His first six-song EP, produced by Anderson, introduced Yoakam to the record business at the nuts-and-bolts level. He even codesigned the jacket and carried the artwork to the typesetter. "I wanted it to look like those early albums I saw when I was a kid," he says. The EP got Yoakam and his group, the Babylonian Cowboys, on the road, which led to a deal with the Halsey agency, which in turn led to Warner Bros.' door. He was signed in November 1985, and Warners

opposite Buck 'n' Dwight: a father-and-son act.

bankrolled some additional sessions to flesh out the EP. Yoakam headed for Capitol studios. "That's where Buck cut, where Merle cut," he says. "It was our connection to our predecessors in west coast country music." Yoakam's spikiness and immodesty were the precise antithesis of the shake 'n' howdy tradition that country singers were supposed to uphold, but beneath the punk veneer lay a very real concern about country music (a well-justified concern considering that Marie Osmond was at number one on the week he broke through). His songs proved that he'd mastered the importance of detail in songwriting. "I'm preoccupied with details because they're the catalysts for life's journey," he says obscurely. "Chuck Berry is *the* genius of everyday life-detail chronicling. He's the poet of the hamburger stand: 'The coolerator was crammed with TV dinners and ginger ale.' How cool! That's brilliant writing! The eloquent articulation of commonplace details."

Yoakam's reputation got a boost when he coaxed Buck Owens out of retirement to form a

above Lyle Lovett.
opposite Steve Earle.

father-and-son act. Owens had retired into self-imposed exile in Bakersfield, and says that Yoakam persuaded him that there was still a place for him in country music. Their relationship was cemented with a joint number one hit, "The Streets of Bakersfield." It was Yoakam's first number one—and Owens's first since 1972. Yoakam has branched into movies (most notably opposite Billy Bob Thornton in *Slingblade*), but no one has ever cared more desperately about country music. As with the Okies, the years in California brought his roots into sharper focus. While most singers wait for their A&R man to make the rounds of the music publishers to find songs, Yoakam sits in his canyon in Los Angeles and writes his own.

Steve Earle and Lyle Lovett had immeasurably less impact on the way country music is made. Lovett had more affinity for archaic jazz, and formed a swing band as soon as he could afford to do so. Earle has been a chameleon throughout his nearly thirty-year career. He has been a coffee-house performer in Texas and a custom songwriter in Nashville; and he has explored traditional country, major label country, metal, Irish music, and more. There's an edgy core to his music, but, as wide as he has roamed, his greatest work is probably that on his first LP from 1986, *Guitar Town*. Emory Gordy and Richard Bennett's production was nuevo rockabilly at its finest, and Earle's songs were populated by a cast of grifters and drifters, always looking for the highway out of town. His well-publicized addiction to cocaine and heroin led to incarceration in the fall of 1994, but release and rehab did not result in a kinder, gentler Steve Earle. In 2002, he released "John Walker's Blues," a sympathetic, perhaps overly sympathetic, portrait of the American Taliban fighter, John Walker Lindh.

Chapter 18

BRANSON, *Missouri*

By the late 1980s, country stars who had been household names for ten, twenty, or thirty years suddenly didn't feel at home in Nashville anymore. The industry became very aware of Country Music Television, and older stars suddenly found themselves without recording contracts and off the radio. They knew they were still popular because they drew well out on the road.

Where could yesterday's heroes go if Nashville didn't want them? The answer turned out to be Branson, Missouri. For the artists, Branson was a godsend. Many had been on the road for as long as they could remember, and Branson meant that, during the summer months at least, they could work every day without traveling. The fans were known as the "RV (recreational vehicle) crowd." They were retired or thinking about retirement, and hadn't been inside a record store in decades.

Looking a little deeper, Branson wasn't quite the surprise it seemed. In 1954, Red Foley left Nashville's *Grand Ole Opry* to start the rival *Ozark Jubilee* in Springfield, Missouri—thirty-five miles north of Branson. The *Jubilee* became the first nationally televised country music show, and ran until 1960. Branson was just starting to become popular as a tourist destination during the years that the *Jubilee* was on the air. Between 1913 and 1958, the White River was dammed in three places, creating three lakes, and in 1960 a gold-rush era theme park, Silver Dollar City, was built nearby. The Branson music scene started in 1959 when the four Mabe brothers began calling themselves the

above Red Foley.
opposite Branson, Missouri.

Baldknobbers and put on regular shows at the Branson community center. The crowds were good, and in 1965 they converted the local skating rink into a theater. Then, in 1968, they built an 850-seat theater. A year earlier, another local act, Presleys' Mountain Music Jubilee, built a low-rise building in the same area. From that point, the scene slowly expanded. In 1983, *Hee-Haw* star Roy Clark became the first name act to open a theater there.

Then, in 1990 and 1991, Branson exploded. Andy Williams, Glen Campbell, Ray Stevens, Tony Orlando, Bobby Vinton, Mel Tillis, and Mickey Gilley opened theaters. *People* magazine did a feature in 1991, and CBS-TV's *60 Minutes* came to town. At its peak in the mid-1990s, some 6 million visitors crowded Branson's narrow roads. There were jokes at Nashville's expense ("Last one out of Nashville, turn out the lights"), but the fact remained that the 6 million or so who flocked to Branson still didn't buy records and still weren't interested in new music. Branson wasn't what Bakersfield had been a generation earlier, and never would be. More than anything, it was a feast in honor of the old way of doing things. Back in the old days, entertainers entertained. They told jokes and stuck around after the show to meet the fans. That became the Branson way. Gary Presley of the Presleys' Mountain Music Jubilee (latterly Presleys' Country Jubilee) told the *Washington Post*, "Doing a straight concert here doesn't work. People want the performers to give a lot of themselves."

right First one out of Nashville: Red Foley boards a plane bound for the Ozarks.

Chapter 19

ALTERNATIVE
and Beyond

Nearly every major change in country music started as alternative country, but the new artists and new sounds were eventually co-opted into the mainstream. Whether the same will be true of the current alternative country bands remains to be seen. In all likelihood, they'll remain apart: mainstream country doesn't want them, and the feeling is mutual.

Just as new traditionalism is often dated to coincide with the first albums by Randy Travis and Dwight Yoakam, so the arrival of alternative country is usually dated to Uncle Tupelo's 1990 album *No Depression*, which took its title and its desolate spirit from the Carter Family's 1936 song, and its inchoate anger from punk. The album title was appropriated by an Internet chat room and magazine, which in turn seemed to give focus to a movement that didn't belong to one geographical area, one record label, or even one continent. It was also the first time that the Internet had played a role in promoting anything that could remotely be called country music.

The godhead of alternative country was Gram Parsons, who, like Hank Williams, became a prophet with honor by dying before he made any egregiously bad records. Some might say that Parsons hadn't done anything radically new and that others had been there before him, including former teen idol Rick Nelson (whose 1966 album *Bright Lights and Country Music* and its 1967 follow-up, *Country Fever*, would have been hailed as country rock's first classics, had anyone heard them). But image is everything, and U2 made a pilgrimage to the site of Parsons' death in the Mojave Desert, not the site of Nelson's death in DeKalb, Texas. Like Hank Williams, Parsons became a blank

above Gram Parsons.
opposite Lambchop.

slate upon which all manner of fantasies could be etched. His musical tastes were almost certainly far more traditional than any of those who invoke his name, stay at his favorite hotels, or take his favorite drugs.

More than anything, alternative country became a pigeonhole for the unclassifiable. Nashville's Lambchop (hailed by their publicist as "Nashville's most fucked-up country band") mixed country, lounge, soul, jazz, and baroque music, underpinning it all with surreal wit. They cited Tammy Wynette and Charlie Rich's producer, Billy Sherrill, as their idols. Sherrill, of course, had been alternative country in his day, bringing lush strings to the Nashville musical palette. But, for all that they might wish it otherwise, Lambchop remain far more visible overseas than at home.

Some tried to make the connection to earlier country more explicit. Former Lambchop member Paul Burch crafted a handful of melodic, whimsical albums, and many of his songs sounded as if they could have been hits in 1962. Gillian Welch's first album, *Revival*, reached even further back: it was the spirit of Carter Stanley made flesh in the 1990s. Welch dressed as if she'd stepped from 1930s' Farm Security Administration photos, and it would be easy to dismiss her work as a Hollywood take on hillbilly music were the songs not so good and so true to the spirit of mountain music. Dale Watson perfected the hillbilly shuffle and paid tribute to truck-driving songs, but he too remained more popular overseas. No one, though, truly loves country music—its pain and its tutti-frutti looniness—more than Robbie Fulks. His record label dubbed him "insurgent country," but at its core his music is rooted in the hardest of hard country music. He tried playing the major label game with one album on Geffen, but returned to the indies.

His tribute album, *13 Hillbilly Giants*, bypassed all the Hanks, Cash, Haggard, and Jones in favor of artists known only to a few, such as Jimmy Murphy, Jimmy Arnold, Wynn Stewart, and Dave Rich. "Monomaniacally fixed on their work and unapologetically true to their strange selves, they seemed to have missed the announcement that there is a certain way of doing things," Fulks wrote in the album liner notes, and he seems destined to follow their example.

The alternative country moment came in 2001 when Wilco, an offshoot of the long-disbanded Uncle Tupelo, submitted an album, *Yankee, Hotel, Foxtrot*, to their label, Warner-Reprise Records. Reprise wanted a rethink, demanding something that radio might find a little friendlier. Wilco frontman Jeff Tweedy refused, and Reprise gave him the tapes as a parting gift. The band posted the album on its website and registered 300,000 hits before another branch of Warner Bros., Nonesuch Records, bought it. "If anybody at a Time Warner board meeting actually looks at the fine print of a report, they'll find they paid for our record twice," said Tweedy. "Which doesn't bother me if it doesn't bother them." In the debacle surrounding *Yankee, Hotel, Foxtrot* we see the artistic paralysis gripping the major labels, resulting in an unwillingness to take risks, and we see 2 million people looking for something that the mainstream music industry isn't delivering.

opposite Gram Parsons, the original cosmic cowboy.

Chapter 20

STADIUM
Country

In mid-April 1989, a tastefully blue and deceptively placid-looking CD hit the stores. It was titled simply *Garth Brooks*. The industry was buzzing over a new Texan singer, Clint Black, but Brooks' first single, "Much Too Young to Feel This Damn Old," reached a respectable number eight. The follow-up, "If Tomorrow Never Comes," went all the way to number one.

Brooks' achievement still paled beside that of Clint Black, whose first four singles went to number one and whose debut LP topped the country charts for twenty-eight weeks. Black looked like new traditionalism's great white hope, while Garth Brooks looked like a quirky performer with an ear for a great song. Brooks' second album, *No Fences*, confirmed that he could handle a broad range of material from wordy ballads to honky-tonk, but no one could have foreseen what would happen next.

The album's first single was a romping bar-room anthem, "Friends in Low Places," but the next release was "The Thunder Rolls." In May 1991, just after "The Thunder Rolls" was released, the industry standard *Billboard* magazine began using a new technology to compile its charts. Earlier charts had been subject to manipulation and represented not only a degree of guesswork, but a bias toward major markets. A company called SoundScan began collecting barcode data from store checkouts to provide a more realistic picture of what was actually selling. Initially, some chains such as Tower Records and most independent stores did not contribute, so the early SoundScan-based charts

above Clint Black.
opposite Clint Black doing the meet 'n' greet at Fan Fair.

reflected sales in chains such as Wal-Mart and thus a bias toward America's heartland. The result was that, after years of being under-reflected, country music was suddenly over-reflected in the national charts. Thirty-four of the top 200 pop albums were country. There was a sudden buzz around country music, and Garth Brooks' "The Thunder Rolls" proved to be just the right song to introduce an entire generation to what was quickly dubbed "new" country. It was literate, melodic, and video-friendly. Brooks portrayed an evil wife-beater in the video, and CMT's refusal to air it only stoked the controversy and the sales. SoundScan eventually refined its technology, bringing Tower and other independents on-line, but by then, Garth Brooks was a mega-star and country music was the most popular music and the most popular radio format in the United States. *No Fences* reached number three on *Billboard*'s pop charts, despite the fact that Capitol had priced it a dollar above the usual country retail price, and Brooks' third album, *Ropin' the Wind*, made its debut on the pop charts at number one in September 1991, despite the fact that Capitol added yet another dollar. That year, Brooks accounted for an estimated 25–30 percent of country record sales, and the total sales of his first three albums exceeded 30 million. His 1992 and 1993 albums, *The Chase* and *In Pieces*, didn't recapture those giddy heights, but ten years on his 2002 album, *Scarecrow*, still topped the country charts and sold over 3 million copies.

Garth Brooks positioned himself astutely between the rage of rap and grunge and the blandness of contemporary pop. He was an astute self-marketer: he had, after all, been an advertising major at Oklahoma State University, and was quick to apply what he'd learned to his own career. His country music pedigree was equally solid: his

mother, Colleen Carroll, had been on Red Foley's *Ozark Jubilee* during the late 1950s, and had recorded for two small labels. Initially, Brooks' musical preferences ran no further than 1970s' rock; he particularly liked the theatrical British band Queen. Witnessing their concert in Oklahoma City, he found himself standing on his seat. "I stood up with my fist high in the air," he said later. "I screamed so loud I could feel the veins in my neck. I was feeling, 'Bring me anything in the world that hasn't been done by mankind. I want to take a crack at it right this second.'" He tried his luck in Nashville in 1985, only to head back to Oklahoma within a day. He returned two years later and found a believer in a man named Bob Doyle, who quit his position at ASCAP's Nashville office to start a publishing company with Brooks as his first client. In 1988, Jim Foglesong at Capitol's Nashville office signed Brooks and entrusted him to veteran songwriter-producer Allen Reynolds, a Memphian who had written "Five o'Clock World" for the Vogues back in the 1960s. At the time, Reynolds was producing Emmylou Harris and the folk-influenced Kathy Mattea, so Capitol clearly saw Brooks along those lines. Shortly after Brooks' breakthrough, though, Foglesong was ousted in favor of the more abrasive Jimmy Bowen, who had been a rockabilly singer and a producer for Frank Sinatra's Reprise Records before arriving in Nashville. Bowen promptly fired Lynn Shults, the A&R man who had seen Brooks perform and suggested that Foglesong sign him. Bowen's aggressiveness made him hugely unpopular in Nashville, but most of his artists liked working with him because he was tenaciously on their side. The exception was Garth Brooks. Bowen had turned down Brooks when he was heading MCA Nashville, and Brooks hadn't forgotten it. Brooks didn't like the fact that Shults had been fired, and that Bowen had turned down his friend Trisha Yearwood.

Things only got worse as sales got better. Brooks demanded a higher royalty, reportedly in the Michael Jackson range of 30 percent, and wanted total creative control that extended to ownership of his masters. In March 1995, he expedited Bowen's exit from Capitol. The tail was wagging the dog, and it was an extraordinary sight. Capitol-EMI's weakness in North America meant that, in 1997, Brooks was able to insist upon the dismissal of Bowen's successor, Scott Hendricks, and then handpick his own president of Capitol Nashville. Brooks' choice was a beer marketer, Pat Quigley, who reportedly looked at Patsy Cline's sales and wondered aloud about the possibility of getting her for a duet session.

Garth Brooks made several wrongheaded moves (he thought he could be a baseball player and tried out for the San Diego Padres, and thought he could president of Capitol Nashville by proxy, and thought

opposite Garth Brooks, a new kind of cowboy.

he could be a rock star named Chris Gaines) but his inalienable contribution to country music was in reformulating the country music show. He brought the trappings of arena rock to country music: dramatic lighting, rear-screen projection, Tarzan-like swinging from ropes, Tarzan-like chest-beating, and tearing back and forth across the stage. His enthusiasm and energy were contagious. Even his detractors had to admit that he put on a hell of a show. It had been seventy years since the Carter Family pulled into small Appalachian towns in their family sedan, posted their little "This Program Is Morally Good" flyers around town, and played to a handful of people in the schoolhouse. Garth Brooks had an advance crew of between sixty and eighty workers setting up his stages, and moved his show from stadium to stadium in twenty trucks and buses.

The other artists who achieved their breakthroughs in 1989–90 were understandably compared with Garth Brooks, whether the comparison was merited or not. Alan Jackson, Clint Black, Travis Tritt, Marty Stuart, and Vince Gill cared deeply about where country music had been and where it was going. Gill and Stuart in particular cemented themselves to the music's past while trying to remain current. Until he sold it in 2002, Stuart had the world's best-stocked private collection of country memorabilia (Hank Williams' suits to Ernest Tubb's bus), but seemed frustrated by the fact that the industry often appeared more interested in his collection than his music.

Vince Gill, like Stuart, is a virtuoso musician. As a teenager, he played in a rock band, and realized one of Garth Brooks' dreams when he opened for Kiss. He was a bluegrass musician and fronted a country rock band, Pure Prairie League, before launching his solo career on RCA in 1984. For several years, he was only fleetingly successful and paid the rent by working sessions as a guitarist or harmony vocalist. It wasn't until he signed with MCA in 1989 that his career began to take off. A song of almost unbearable loss, "When I Call Your Name," reached only number two, but won the CMA award as Single of the Year. Vince Gill proved himself the master of the country ballad: he had the poise, the sense of drama, and the ability to sing slowly without letting the tension falter. He can sing softly with almost embarrassing intimacy, yet soar with Orbison-like range and control.

Alan Jackson decided early to take his stand with bedrock country music, and it has paid off handsomely for him. He went to Nashville in an old pickup truck and worked in the Opryland mailroom until he landed a songwriting contract and then a recording deal with the newly formed Nashville branch of Arista Records. His debut, *Here in the Real World*, was hardcore, real-life country music, and his subsequent albums have stayed true to that credo. The characters in his songs like fast cars, a few beers on a hot night, weekends out at someone's place on the water, a woman to love, and a few acres. They don't understand much of what happens outside their home town, much less the world. Alan Jackson quietly takes a stand. At the 1999 CMA awards, the Association wanted George Jones to sing a fragment of his song "Choices." Jones was upset at having his number curtailed and refused to appear at all. Jackson was scheduled to sing his hit "Pop a Top," but a little way into the song he abruptly switched to "Choices," sang the entire song, then exited the building. Later, he and George Strait teamed up on a stinging indictment of current

country music, "Murder on Music Row." And then, in 2001, Jackson sang his song about the World Trade Center atrocity, "Where Were You When the World Stopped Turning?" To many outside the United States, it was simplistic, almost xenophobic, but it perfectly mirrored the way the tragedy played out in smaller towns across the country. He sang it alone with his guitar at the 2001 CMA awards, and a nation wept.

As the 1990s came to a close, one artist towered over country music. She didn't live in Nashville; in fact, she didn't even live in the United States any more. With American sales approaching 20 million, Shania Twain's *Come on Over* is the most successful country album of all time, but, if presented as a potential screenplay, her story would be dubbed too strange to be credible. She was born Eileen Edwards across the river from Detroit in the Canadian city of Windsor. Her mother left her father, married an Ojibway indian, and moved far north to the bleak, bitter cold of Timmins, Ontario. Eileen changed her name to Shania and took her stepfather's name, Twain. She began performing in the resort lodges south of Timmins and appeared on Canadian television. Then, in 1986, Twain's mother and stepfather were killed in a road accident, and she raised her younger siblings for a few years before deciding to take another crack at the music business.

In 1991, she went to Nashville and was signed by Mercury Records. The first album was a paint-by-numbers Nashville record, and its only merit was that a video accompanying the first single was seen by the Zimbabwean record producer Mutt Lange, who'd produced AC/DC, Def Leppard, and Bryan Adams. Lange wanted to produce Twain's second album, *The Woman in Me*, and halfway through the lengthy production they married. Mercury's Nashville division had just been taken over by Luke Lewis who

opposite Alan Jackson.

had worked in pop music promotion and was less scared of what Lange proposed to spend than many around Nashville might have been. Lewis admired Lange's ability to insert a "hook" into a song "every couple of seconds or so," but Lange's real contribution was his reinvention of the country mix. The fiddle and steel guitar were there, but framed as if on a rock record. Lewis then committed the funds necessary to promote the record. They scrapped one video and redid another, taking full advantage of Twain's wholesome farm-girl sexuality. Warner Bros. Records was promoting its new signee Faith Hill with a pin-up calendar, and Mercury did likewise. Ads appeared in *Sports Illustrated* and other magazines that didn't ordinarily reach country fans.

Twain sold to women, who liked her feisty independence, and to men, who adored her sexuality. She refused to tour to support the album, but sales rocketed ever upward, thus confounding conventional wisdom. Twain, meanwhile, was writing her third album with Lange, and the sales of *Come on Over* exceeded all expectations. The album was remixed and redesigned for territories outside the USA, and topped charts all across Europe. She finally toured, mounting a live show that equaled Garth Brooks'. "Rural people have satellite dishes in their backyards," Luke Lewis told journalist Clark Parsons. "They see commercials that cost a million bucks, they see exciting visual images constantly, but there seems to be some tendency—because country music is rooted so deeply—to try to hang onto the sensibility that our audience is backward in some way. Consumers of country music are sophisticated. To keep pace with that, [your video] mustn't look like it was made ten

left But is it country? Shania Twain.

years ago." Shania Twain and Mutt Lange retreated to Switzerland and started a family. Her fourth album would not come until it was ready.

The new millennium was not a happy dawn for the country music business, or for the music business in general. Country's share of recorded music sales slipped from an all-time high of 18.7 percent in 1993 to an eleven-year low of 10.5 percent in 2001, and the bad news was compounded by the fact that the pie itself was getting measurably smaller. Music sales fell by 6 percent in 2001, and plunged even more precipitously in 2002. The industry blamed Internet piracy and the economic downturn, but the causes were more deepseated. Music as a commodity had cheapened itself by becoming ubiquitous, and there seemed to be an all-pervasive lack of interest in any new artist, regardless of genre. In country, the most frequent complaint was that the artists looked and sounded the same. The record companies admitted it, but were powerless to do much about it. The artistic paradigm had been turned on its head.

In earlier times, the artist would come to the A&R man with his songs or songs he'd found. The A&R man would throw his own choices into the ring, and they'd make the record. It would be delivered to the promotion department (which would take it to radio) and to the sales department (which would take it to retail). The stakes were low. If a single failed, the company was out-of-pocket a few hundred dollars in recording costs and a few thousand dollars in pressing and distribution costs and overheads.

Now, with the stakes so much higher, the artistic equation has been reversed. It all starts with radio. The goal of the biggest radio stations is to prevent the "tune-out" when the consumer switches stations, and to that end, the stations program a

mix that varies within very narrow parameters. In order to reach the major stations, the record labels will concentrate on music within those same narrow parameters. The promotion department, which once had no vote in what got released, now has the biggest vote because the company has so much money at risk. After signing bonuses, pre-production, production, video, and promotion it's unusual for a record to hit the streets with less than half a million dollars invested. With that kind of money on the line, record companies put out a call for songs that fit within radio's narrow parameters, and the songwriters naturally write songs that they think will be cut. Even the technique of writing songs has changed. They're almost invariably cowritten today, and this too has affected the music. Most of the great country songs—"The Last Letter," "Dusty Skies," "I'm So Lonesome I Could Cry," "Walking the Floor Over You," "I Love You a Thousand Ways," "Oh, Lonesome Me," "Flowers on the Wall"—seemed to be snapshots of one man or one woman's feelings on one night, often one dark night. Cowritten songs lack that immediacy. They tend to be confections, painstakingly crafted, and endlessly refined.

Inevitably, newer country artists cannot hear all that their predecessors heard or see all their predecessors saw. Some might have a close relative with a large traditional country collection, but most grew up with 1980s' rock. In fact, the production values of 1970s' and '80s' rock seem to drive current country music. Of the new bloods, Kenny Chesney sings Stevie Ray Vaughan's "Pride and Joy" and Billy Joel's "You May Be Right," Tim McGraw sings Dan Fogelberg's "Leader of the Band," and Garth Brooks' infatuation with the Kiss era went as far as an ill-considered rock album released pseudonymously. Talking to journalist Tom Roland,

Trisha Yearwood said, "AC/DC would be a stretch for me, but if you talk about artists like Bob Seger, John Mellencamp, James Taylor, the Eagles, and Stevie Nicks, [Linda] Ronstadt…that whole period of stuff, late '70s [to] early '80s, where the songs have a story to tell…that music today is having a hard time finding a home, and country music's in a state of transition."

It's true. Country music *is* in a state of transition, but it has *always* been in a state of transition. Back in the nineteenth century, there were probably complaints when local mountain balladeers began singing contemporary pop songs or music-hall songs. Jimmie Rodgers sang black music and Patsy Cline sang pop music, and both were criticized for it. Commentators say that at critical points in its history country music has rediscovered its inalienable countriness, and that may be the case again, but the fact remains that the two biggest country stars of the 1990s—Garth Brooks and Shania Twain—did not recapture the countriness in country music. The record that reclaimed the countriness was the soundtrack to *O Brother, Where Art Thou*, which featured songs written at various points between the 1800s and 1935, and sold millions of copies. It had the industry scratching its head because it was traditional country music, but it wasn't selling to the current country audience. *O Brother* wasn't even a country record if "country" meant current country music. It was the United States rediscovering itself through old, quintessentially American music at a time when its values and its soil were under attack. The songs of death and walking spirits underscored the emotional poverty of the Nashville product, and the fiddle and banjo enabled a new generation to reconnect with the time when America was struggling to carve out its own identity.

At its heart, country music is the sound of Americans making music for Americans. Jazz and blues had parochial origins, but erased cultural barriers to become worldwide currencies. Country music has not. In fact, it might be at its best when it's specific to the United States. Throughout its history, it has mirrored the country's growth and aspirations.

Country music is the backwoods piety and rude ambition of the Carter Family and the rowdiness of Jimmie Rodgers. It's the fierce drive of Bill Monroe's brand of bluegrass and it's Ernest Tubb giving a voice to returning servicemen. It's Hank Williams' and Johnny Cash's dark soliloquies, and the defiant bubbaness of Hank, Jr. and Travis Tritt. Country music isn't the music of the hills or even the South anymore. It's playing in all the places that the tourists don't go: strip malls, stock-car meets, Wal-Mart, back country lakes, tiny highways, and small-town diners. It's America's century in microcosm.

lifelines

This section provides additional biographical information about the principal people in the text in order of mention. It also offers suggestions for further reading and further listening.

INTRODUCTION
Dock Boggs—born West Norton, Virginia, February 7, 1898; died Norton, Virginia, February 7, 1971. Rediscovered in 1963 by folklorist Mike Seeger, and played folk festivals.

Further Reading
CD booklet to Dock Boggs, *Country Blues* (Revenant Records, 1997)
Malone, Bill C., *Don't Get Above Your Raisin': Country Music and the Southern Working Class* (University of Illinois Press, Champaign, 2002)

CHAPTER 1
Alan Lomax—born Austin, Texas, January 31, 1915; died July 19, 2002. Folklorist, writer, and film-maker who traveled throughout the world, writing and recording prolifically.

The Blue Sky Boys—Bill Bolick, born Hickory, North Carolina, October 28, 1917. Earl Bolick, born Hickory, NC, November 16, 1919; died April 19, 1998. They retired in 1951, believing that their time had passed, but the folk revival inspired them to regroup occasionally.

Eck Robertson—born Madison Co., Arkansas, November 20, 1887; died February 17, 1975.

Further Reading
Lomax, Alan, *Southern Journey: The Alan Lomax Collection* (notes to CD series, Rounder Records, 1997)
Lomax, Alan, *Folk Songs of North America* (Doubleday, New York, 1960)
Malone, Bill C., *Country Music U.S.A.* (University of Texas Press, Austin, 2002)
Malone, Bill C., *Cowboys and Musical Mountaineers,* revised edition (University of Georgia Press, Athens, 1994)
Millard, Andre, *America on Record: A History of Recorded Sound* (Cambridge University Press, New York, 1995)

Further Listening
In 1997, Rounder Records began a projected 100-volume series of

THE BLUE SKY BOYS

Lomax's field work. The *Southern Journey* sub-set includes the Appalachian recordings. Check out Rounder's website or catalog for the appropriate volumes. The Blue Sky Boys' classic RCA recordings are unavailable. Two comeback LPs, *In Concert '64* (1989) and *The Blue Sky Boys* (1984), are available on Rounder. There's a Louvin Brothers sampler, *When I Stop Dreaming* (Razor + Tie Records, 1995), and their complete recordings are in an eight-CD box, *Close Harmony* (Bear Family Records, 1992). The Everly Brothers' classic country brother duet album, *Songs Our Daddy Taught Us,* is widely available on many labels.

CHAPTER 2
Ralph Peer—born Kansas City, Missouri, May 22, 1892; died, January 19, 1960. The company he founded, now called Peermusic, is one of the largest independent music publishers in the world.

The Carter Family—Alvin Pleasant (A. P.), born Maces Spring, Virginia, December 15, 1891; died November 7, 1960. Sara Carter, born Flat Woods, Virginia, July 21, 1899; died January 8, 1975; Maybelle Carter, born Nickelville, Virginia, May 10, 1909;

THE CARTER FAMILY

died, October 23, 1978. Maybelle and her daughters, June, Anita, and Helen, kept the family act alive. Maybelle and the Carter Sisters worked with Johnny Cash from 1961, and the sisters stayed with Cash after Maybelle's death.

Jimmie Rodgers—birthplace unknown (usually assumed to be Meridian, Mississippi, but other sources say Geiger, Alabama), September 8, 1897; died in New York during a break in recording sessions, May 26, 1933.

Vernon Dalhart—born Marion Try Slaughter in Jefferson, Texas, April 6, 1883; died September 15, 1948.

Further Reading
Porterfield, Nolan, *Jimmie Rodgers: The Life and Times of America's Blue Yodeler* (University of Illinois Press, Champaign, 1992)
Wolfe, Charles, "The Bristol Sessions Revisited" in *The Country Reader*, ed. Paul Kingsbury (Vanderbilt University Press, Nashville, 1996)
Wolfe, Charles, boxed set notes to *The Carter Family: In the Shadow of Clinch Mountain* (Bear Family Records, 2000)
Zwonitzer, Mark and Hirshberg,

Charles, *Will You Miss Me When I'm Gone? The Carter Family and Their Legacy in Country Music* (Simon & Schuster, New York, 2002)

Further Listening
Rounder Records reissued all of Jimmie Rodgers' recordings (eight volumes, 1991) and all of the Carter Family's RCA recordings (nine volumes, 1991-9). MCA Nashville reissued a selection of the Carters' Decca recordings (*The Country Music Hall of Fame*, 1992). Bear Family's twelve-CD Carter Family set, *In the Shadow of Clinch Mountain* (2000), is the motherlode, though, comprising every recording by the original Carter Family together with a book that includes lyric transcriptions, a biography, and every known photograph. Bear Family's Jimmie Rodgers six-CD set, *The Singing Brakeman* (1992), is similarly comprehensive. There are many single-CD best-of Rodgers collections, the most recent being RCA's 2002 set, *Country Legends*. The Country Music Hall of Fame reissued all of the recordings that Ralph Peer made in Bristol in 1927 (including all those *not* by Rodgers and the Carter Family) on *The Bristol Sessions*, 1987.

CHAPTER 3
Arthur Satherley—born Bristol, England, October 19, 1889; fired from Columbia Records in 1952, and died in Los Angeles, February 10, 1986. In addition to his country signings, Satherley also recorded blues giant Robert Johnson.

Bob Wills—born James Robert Wills in Kosse, Texas, March 6, 1905; died May 13, 1975.

Tommy Duncan—born Hillsboro, Texas, January 11, 1911; died July 23, 1967.

Milton Brown—born Stephenville, Texas, September 8, 1903; died April 18, 1936 as the result of a car wreck.

Gene Autry—born Orvon Gene Autry in Tioga, Texas, September 29, 1907; died October 2, 1998. In addition to his role as America's preeminent singing cowboy, Autry also launched several music publishing companies, a record label (Challenge Records), and owned the California Angels baseball team, several hotels, and had vast real estate holdings.

GENE AUTRY

Roy Rogers—born Leonard Slye in Cincinnati, Ohio, November 5, 1911; died July 6, 1998. The other original Sons of the Pioneers were Robert Nobles (Bob Nolan), born New Brunswick, Canada, April 1, 1908; died, June 16, 1980, and Vernon Tim Spencer, born Webb City, Missouri, July 13, 1908; died April 26, 1974.

Further Reading

Ginell, Cary, *Milton Brown and the Founding of Western Swing* (University of Illinois Press, Champaign, 1994)
Logsdon, Guy, *The Whorehouse Bells Were Ringing* (University of Illinois Press, Champaign, 1995)
Townsend, Charles, *San Antonio Rose* (University of Illinois Press, Champaign, 1986)

Further Listening

Columbia's *Essential Bob Wills* (1992) is just that, and Rhino has an equally good career-spanning overview, *1935-1973* (1991), while Bear Family has the complete Columbia recordings in a twelve-CD box, *San Antonio Rose* (2000). Milton Brown's work is available only on the five-CD *Complete Recordings* (Texas Rose Records, 1995). Rhino has a western swing anthology that makes a good starting point, *Heroes of Country Music Vol.1: Legends of Western Swing* (1995).

The best Gene Autry overview is *The Essential* (Columbia, 1992), and his earlier recordings are on *Blues Singer 1929-1931* (Columbia, 1996). The Sons of the Pioneers' classic recordings, including those with Roy Rogers, are on *Ultimate Collection* (Hip-O, 2001). Rhino issued a four-CD box, *Happy Trails—The Roy Rogers Collection 1937-1990* (1996), but the best starting point for an overview of western music is a four-volume Rounder set, *Singing in the Saddle (Seventy Years of Recorded Cowboy Music)*, 1996.

CINDY WALKER

CHAPTER 4

Cindy Walker—born Mart, Texas, July 20, 1918. Her grandfather was hymn writer F. P. Eiland ("Hold to God's Unchanging Hand"). In 1954, she returned to Texas to live with her mother, and retired to the family home in Mexia.

Rex Griffin—born Gadsden, Alabama, August 12, 1912; died in a charity hospital in New Orleans, October 7, 1958.

Further Reading

Coffey, Kevin, boxed set notes to *Rex Griffin—The Last Letter* (Bear Family Records, 1996)
Passman, Arnold, *The Dee-Jays* (Macmillan, New York, 1971)
Sanjek, Russell and Sanjek, David, *American Popular Music Business in the Twentieth Century* (Oxford University Press, New York, 1991)

Further Listening

Rex Griffin's recordings are available only on a three-CD boxed set, *The Last Letter* (Bear Family Records, 1996).

CHAPTER 5

Jimmie Davis—birthdate uncertain, but usually accepted as September 11, 1899; died November 5, 2000. He was twice governor of Louisiana (1944-8 and 1960-4), and recorded religious music late in life.

Al Dexter—born Albert Poindexter in Troup, Texas, May 4, 1905; died January 28, 1984. He became a club owner in Texas and retired in the 1960s.

Floyd Tillman—born Ryan, Oklahoma, December 8, 1914, but grew up in Texas. In addition to "It Makes No Difference Now," "Slipping Around," and "This Cold War with You," Tillman wrote another major hit, "I Love You So Much It Hurts" (recorded by Red Foley, Andy Williams, Jerry Lee Lewis, and many others). He became a hero in the Austin music scene, and still plays occasionally.

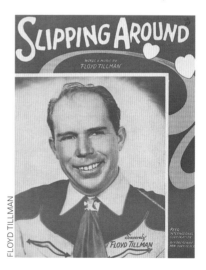

FLOYD TILLMAN

Ernest Tubb—born Crisp, Texas, February 9, 1914; died September 6, 1984. He moved to Nashville in 1943, and became one of the most respected elder statesmen in country music. In 1947, he opened Ernest Tubb's Record Shop, perhaps the first all-country music record store. Tubb mail-ordered records across the nation. He scored hits from 1941 until 1979.

Further Reading
Pugh, Ronnie, *Ernest Tubb: The Texas Troubadour* (Duke University Press, Durham, North Carolina, 1998)
Tosches, Nick, *Country* (Da Capo Press, New York, 1996)

Further Listening
There's a single CD Jimmie Davis overview, *Country Music Hall of Fame* (MCA Nashville, 1993), but the earlier blues recordings are only on a four-CD set, *Nobody's Darlin' but Mine* (Bear Family, 1998). Al Dexter's "Pistol Packin' Mama" is on the excellent anthology *Heroes of Country Music Vol.2: Legends of Honky Tonk* (Rhino, 1995). Floyd Tillman's finest work is on *The Best of Floyd Tillman* (Collectors Choice Music, 1998). There are two good Ernest Tubb overviews: *The Country Music Hall of Fame* (MCA Nashville, 1992) and a double CD, *Definitive Hits* (Collectors Choice, 2001). Bear Family goes deeper, reissuing his complete recordings for RCA and Decca/MCA on five boxed sets—a total of thirty CDs (1991-9). Check out their catalog or website for full details.

CHAPTER 6
Bill Monroe—born Rosine, Kentucky, September 13, 1911; died September 9, 1996. Monroe's lean years, beginning with the onset of rock 'n' roll, ended in the mid-1960s when folklorist Ralph Rainzler began

booking him on the college circuit and building festivals around him. In 1967, Monroe launched his own annual festival in Bean Blossom, Indiana. His brother Charlie (born Ohio Co., Kentucky, July 4, 1903) organized a band, the Kentucky Pardners, after splitting from Bill, but he retired to his farm in Kentucky in the mid-1950s. Late in life, he played and recorded again. He died September 27, 1975.

THE STANLEY BROTHERS

The Stanley Brothers—Carter, born Stratton, Virginia, August 27, 1925; and Ralph, also born in Stratton, February 25, 1927. They began playing professionally in 1946, and first recorded in 1947 for the local Rich-R-Tone Records. They brought trio harmonies to bluegrass, and recorded prolifically throughout the 1950s and early 1960s. Carter died December 1, 1966. Ralph carried on, and has enjoyed a second career as a solo attraction much longer than his first as one of the Stanley Brothers.

Flatt & Scruggs—Lester Flatt, born Duncan's Chapel, Tennessee, June 14,

1914, and Earl Scruggs, born Flint Hill, North Carolina, January 6, 1924. Flatt & Scruggs left Monroe in 1948, and stayed together until 1969. Flatt later led his own band, featuring teenaged Marty Stuart on mandolin, until his death on May 11, 1979. Scruggs retired in 1980, although he has recently begun appearing on *The Grand Ole Opry* again.

Alison Krauss—born Decatur, Illinois, July 23, 1971.

Further Reading
Rosenberg, Neil V., *Bluegrass: A History* (University of Illinois Press, Champaign, 1993)
Smith, Richard D., *Can't You Hear Me Callin'? The Life of Bill Monroe* (Da Capo Press, New York, 2001)
Wright, John, *Travelin' the High Way Home* (University of Illinois Press, Champaign, 1995)

Further Listening
Universal's Hip-O label has a two-volume bluegrass primer, *Bluegrass Essentials Volumes 1 and 2* (1998 and 1999). The Monroe Brothers recordings are being issued by Rounder Records on a series of five CDs: the first two are *What Would You Give in Exchange for Your Soul?* (2000) and *Just a Song of Old Kentucky* (2001). Monroe's RCA recordings are on *Country Legends* (2002), and his Columbia recordings are on *The Essential* (1992). In 2002, Bear Family plans to reissue all the RCAs and Columbias in a six-CD boxed set, *1936-1949*, with unissued sides. Between 1989 and 1994, Bear Family reissued most of Monroe's Decca recordings in three boxed sets,

1950-1958, 1959-1969, and *1970-1979*. In 1994, MCA Nashville issued a four-CD career-spanning overview, *The Music of Bill Monroe 1936-1994*, which remains the best starting point.

The Stanley Brothers' recordings are widely available. The Rich-R-Tone recordings are on *Earliest Recordings* (Revenant, 1997), and the classic Columbia sides are on *1949-1952* (Bear Family, 1991) and on *The Complete Columbia Stanley Brothers* (Sony/Columbia, 1996). The equally classic Mercury recordings are available in abbreviated form on *Angel Band* (Mercury Nashville, 1995) and complete on *1953-1958* (Bear Family, 1993). There are several anthologies drawn from the King/Starday recordings, including a four-CD box, *The Early King/Starday Years 1958-1961* (King Records, 1994), and *Riding That Midnight Train* (Westside, 1999).

Flatt & Scruggs' music is also widely available in a variety of configurations. *'Tis Sweet to Be Remembered* (Sony 1997) is a two-CD synopsis of the Columbia years. *The Millennium Collection* (Universal, 2000) samples the early Mercury recordings. Between 1992 and 1995, Bear Family reissued *everything* that Flatt & Scruggs recorded on three boxed sets, *1949-1959, 1959-1963,* and *1964-1969*. The first box is consistently excellent.

CHAPTER 7
Radio station WSM—started in Nashville, October 5, 1925 by the National Life & Accident Company (its call letters stood for We Shield Millions). *The Grand Ole Opry* was launched on November 25, 1925.

In 1927, WSM became affiliated with the NBC radio network. WSM inaugurated the annual Dee-Jay Convention and the annual Fan Fair. National Life sold WSM in 1982, and it is currently owned by Gaylord Corporation. *The Grand Ole Opry* moved from the Ryman Auditorium to a purpose-built theme park, Opryland, in March 1974.

ROY ACUFF

Roy Acuff—born near Maynardville, Tennessee, September 15, 1903; died November 23, 1992. Acuff's career began to falter in the late 1940s, and he was dropped by Columbia Records in 1952. In 1957, he joined Hickory Records (an offshoot of Acuff-Rose Publications, the music publisher he'd cofounded in 1942). He became the first living member of the Country Music Hall of Fame on his induction in 1962. When *The Opry* moved to Opryland, the management built Acuff a house in the grounds.

Further Reading
Kingsbury, Paul, *The Grand Ole Opry History of Country Music* (Villard, New York, 1995)

Wolfe, Charles, *A Good Natured Riot* (Vanderbilt University Press, Nashville, 1999)

Further Listening
Roy Acuff's career has not been properly anthologized in the CD era, although the three-LP set *Country & Western Classics* (Time-Life, 1983) can still be found. The best of the Columbia recordings are on *The Essential 1938-1949* (Columbia, 1992).

CHAPTER 8
Fred Rose—born Evansville, Indiana, August 24, 1898; died December 1, 1954. He moved to Chicago in 1917 and began writing jazz and pop songs. His biggest hits as a songwriter include "Blue Eyes Crying in the Rain," "Deed I Do," "Honest and Truly," "Fireball Mail," "It's a Sin," "Settin' the Woods on Fire," and "Take These Chains from My Heart." In January 1954, he launched Hickory Records.

Hiriam "Hank" Williams—born Mount Olive (West), Alabama, September 17, 1923 and grew up in Georgiana, Greenville, and Montgomery, Alabama. He was a big star in and around Montgomery by the time he began recording in 1946. He died en route to a show in Canton, Ohio, either late in the evening of December 31, 1952 or early on January 1, 1953.

Further Reading
Escott, Colin, Merritt, George, and MacEwen, William, *Hank Williams: the Biography* (Little, Brown, New York, 1995)

HANK WILLIAMS

Florita, Kira and Escott, Colin, *Hank Williams: Snapshots from the Lost Highway* (Da Capo Press, New York, 2001)
Hawkins, Martin, boxed set notes to *A Shot in the Dark: Tennessee Jive* (Bear Family Records, 2000)

Further Listening
The eight-CD boxed set *A Shot in the Dark: Tennessee Jive* (Bear Family, 2000) recounts the early days of the Nashville music business, told from the standpoint of the independent labels. Hank Williams has been exhaustively anthologized from budget CDs to a comprehensive ten-CD boxed set, *The Complete Hank Williams* (Mercury, Nashville, 1998). *Live at the Grand Ole Opry* (Mercury, Nashville 1999) is a two-CD set that gives a sense of Williams on-air, and another two-CD set, *The Health and Happiness Shows* (Mercury, Nashville 1993), collects a series of 1949 radio shows. Old Hank Williams LPs should usually be avoided because they feature overdubbed recordings.

CHAPTER 9

Bullet Records—Nashville's first independent record label (although several gospel artists ran private labels from Nashville). It started in April 1946 and went out of business around 1952, although it was revived periodically. Leon Payne cut the original version of "Lost Highway" for Bullet.

Steve Sholes—born Washington, D.C., February 12, 1911; died April 22, 1968. He joined his father at the RCA plant in Camden, New Jersey, in 1929, becoming head of Pop Singles in 1957 following his success with Elvis Presley. He spent his entire working life in the service of RCA, and died en route to a session in Nashville.

Don Law—born London, England, February 24, 1902; died December 20, 1982. He sang with the London Choral Society and emigrated to the USA in 1924. He was a book-keeper for Vocalion Records in Dallas when ARC (later Columbia) bought Vocalion in 1931, and began working with fellow Englishman Art Satherley. After retiring from Columbia in 1967, he moved to Texas.

Paul Cohen—born Chicago, November 10, 1908: died April 1, 1970. He worked for Columbia Records in the 1920s, then joined Decca when the US operation was opened in 1934. He ran the country division from the mid-1940s onward, then headed Decca's Coral subsidiary in 1958 before leaving to start his own company, Todd Records. In 1964, he joined Kapp Records, and was head of ABC's Nashville division in 1968 and 1969.

Owen Bradley—born Westmoreland, Tennessee, October 21, 1915; died January 7, 1998. He led a society dance band until Paul Cohen recruited him to run Decca's country division. He and his brother Harold opened one of the first independent studios in Nashville. He remained head of Decca Nashville (by then MCA) until 1976, and ran his own studio, Bradley's Barn, in Mt. Juliet, Tennessee.

Ken Nelson—born Caledonia, Minnesota, January 19, 1911. Shortly after he began working for WJJD, Chicago, he was put in charge of their country programming (to that point his background had been classical music). He joined Capitol in 1949, taking over the country music department in 1952, and remained in charge until 1976.

Eddy Arnold—born Henderson, Tennessee, May 15, 1918. He joined Pee Wee King's Golden West Cowboys and was signed to RCA in 1943. He also joined *The Opry* in 1943, but left in 1948 and became the best-selling country artist of the late 1940s. His

DON LAW

career slowed in the 1950s but revived in the 1960s when he began recording crossover pop-country. He recorded until 1998 and retired in 2000.

Clyde "Red" Foley—born Blue Lick, Kentucky, June 17, 1910; died September 19, 1968. He became a star on WLS, Chicago, and moved to *The Opry* in 1946. He was hugely popular in the late 1940s and early 1950s with songs such as "Tennessee Saturday Night" and "Chattanoogie Shoe Shine Boy." In 1953, Foley left *The Opry*, and in 1955 began hosting the first networked country music telecast, *The Ozark Jubilee*. After the show ended in 1960, he returned to Nashville and toured until his death.

Orville "Lefty" Frizzell—born Corsicana, Texas, March 31, 1928; died Nashville, July 19, 1975.

Michael Webb Pierce—born Monroe, Louisiana, August 8, 1921; died Nashville, February 24, 1991. Like Hank Williams, Faron Young, Elvis Presley, Jim Reeves, and Slim Whitman, Pierce launched his career from Shreveport's *Louisiana Hayride*. He began recording for his own Pacemaker Records in 1951, and signed with Decca later that year. He moved to Nashville in 1952.

Clarence "Hank" Snow—born Brooklyn, Nova Scotia, Canada, May 9, 1914; died Nashville, December 20, 1999.

Further Reading
Cooper, Daniel, *Lefty Frizzell* (Little, Brown, New York, 1996)

Hawkins, Martin, boxed set notes to *A Shot in the Dark: Tennessee Jive* (Bear Family Records, 2000)
Snow, Hank, *The Hank Snow Story* (University of Illinois Press, Champaign, 1994)
Streissguth, Michael, *Eddy Arnold: Pioneer of the Nashville Sound* (Schirmer Books, New York, 2001)

Further Listening
Most major artists of the 1940s and 1950s re-recorded their hits during the stereo era, and the remakes usually find their way to cheaper reissues. At Eddy Arnold's insistence, his classic early recordings were never reissued at all, and are available only on a five-CD boxed set, *The Tennessee Plowboy* (Bear Family, 1998). Red Foley's career is sampled on *The Country Music Hall of Fame* (MCA Nashville, 1991).

Lefty Frizzell is poorly represented on single CDs. *The Best of Lefty Frizzell* (Rhino, 1991) includes all his greatest hits, but, as usual, it's up to Bear Family to do the exhaustive complete edition—a monumental twelve-CD set, *Life's Like Poetry* (1992). The only overview of Webb Pierce's career is the

MARTY ROBBINS

Country Music Hall of Fame's *King of the Honky Tonk* (1994). Hank Snow's greatest hits are on *The Essential* (RCA, 1997) and other compilations, but again, beware of remakes. All of his prolific output has been gathered by Bear Family on a series of six boxed sets, totaling thirty-five CDs (1988-94). The first box, *Singing Ranger Vol.1* (1988), catches Snow in his prime, while *The Thesaurus Transcriptions* (1994) features unguarded small-group radio performances.

CHAPTER 10
Marty Robbins—born Martin David Robinson in Glendale, Arizona, September 26, 1925; died Nashville, December 8, 1982. He became a star around Phoenix in the late 1940s, and was signed to Columbia Records in 1951 in a deal that also brought him to *The Grand Ole Opry*. After recording in New York, he returned to country, inaugurating the craze for western songs with "El Paso" in 1960.

Ferlin Husky—born Flat River, Missouri, December 3, 1927. He moved to Bakersfield in 1949 and became one of the founders of the Bakersfield scene. His first hit, "A Dear John Letter," came during the Korean War. Aside from "Gone," his biggest hit was "Wings of a Dove" in 1960.

Sonny James—born James Loden in Hackleburg, Alabama, May 1, 1929. He recorded the original version of the country classic "I Forgot More Than You'll Ever Know," and, after flirting with teen music, returned to country, becoming very successful in the 1970s. He also produced Marie

Osmond's million-seller, "Paper Roses."

Jim Reeves—born Panola Co., Texas, August 20, 1923; died at the controls of a plane, July 31, 1964. A semi-pro baseball player, he became a dee-jay after an injury forced him from the game. He began recording for Macy's in 1949. After joining RCA in 1955, he moved to Nashville from Shreveport, Louisiana. He became hugely popular in Europe and South Africa.

Further Reading
Guralnick, Peter, *Last Train to Memphis: The Rise of Elvis Presley* (Little, Brown, Boston, 1994)
Streissguth, Michael, *Like a Moth to a Flame: The Jim Reeves Story* (Rutledge Hill Press, Nashville, 1998)

Further Listening
Elvis's Sun recordings are complete on *Sunrise* (RCA, 1999). Sonny James's "Young Love" is available on countless anthologies. Ferlin Husky's 1952 version of "Gone" is included alongside the 1956 version on *Vintage Collection* (Capitol Nashville, 1996). The best overview of Marty Robbins' career is the two-CD set *The Essential* (Capitol Nashville, 1992), and his complete New York pop sessions are on Bear Family's 1991 compilation *Rockin' Rollin' Robbins Vol.2 (The Ray Conniff Sessions)*. Jim Reeves' "Four Walls" is available on numberless sets, but RCA's *Essential* (1995) is re-engineered from the original masters.

CHAPTER 11
Alvis "Buck" Owens—born Sherman, Texas, August 12, 1929. His family moved to Arizona in 1937, and

Owens began working the honky-tonks around Phoenix before moving to Bakersfield in 1951. He recorded for small labels, including a rockabilly single issued under the name of "Corky Jones" before joining Capitol in 1956. He became one of the biggest stars of the 1960s, and his song "Act Naturally" was covered by the Beatles. He also hosted the longest-running country music television show, *Hee-Haw* (1969-94).

RAY PRICE

Ray Price—born Perryville, Texas, January 12, 1926. After forsaking the country shuffles in 1967, he began a second career as a lounge entertainer, scoring a huge pop and country smash with Kris Kristofferson's "For the Good Times" in 1970.

Further Reading
Haslam, Gerald, *Working Man Blues* (University of California Press, Berkeley, 1999)

Further Listening
The definitive Bakersfield set has yet to be done. Capitol's out-of-print *Hillbilly Music, Thank God!* (1985) is a starting point, when it can be found,

as is Rhino's 1995 set *Heroes of Country Music Volume 4: Legends of the West Coast* (which includes Joe Maphis's "Dim Lights, Thick Smoke, and Loud, Loud Music"). In 1992, Rhino issued a career-spanning three-CD Buck Owens box, *The Buck Owens Collection 1959-1990*. Tommy Collins' music is available only in a five-CD box, *Leonard* (Bear Family, 1992). Ray Price's classic recordings are on Columbia's 1991 anthology *The Essential 1951-1962*.

CHAPTER 12
Patsy Montana—born Ruby Blevins in Hope, Arkansas, October 30, 1908; died May 3, 1996. She joined an all-female troupe called the Montana Cowgirls and renamed herself Patsy Montana. Her trademark was exuberant yodeling, and she continued working until her death.

Kitty Wells—born Muriel Deason, August 30, 1919. She was one of the few country stars actually from Nashville. She married Johnnie Wright, later half of Johnnie and Jack, in 1937, and worked with them on *Louisiana Hayride*. She began recording in 1949, and was in the charts until 1979. In 2001, she and Wright retired from touring.

Patsy Cline—born Virginia Hensley in Winchester, Virginia, September 8, 1932; died March 5, 1963.

Loretta Lynn—born Loretta Webb in Butcher Holler, Kentucky, April 14, 1935.

Dolly Parton—born Locust Ridge, Tennessee, January 19, 1946.

PATSY CLINE

Tammy Wynette—born Virginia Wynette Pugh in Itawamba Co., Mississippi, May 5, 1942; died Nashville, April 6, 1998.

Further Reading
Jones, Margaret, *Patsy Cline* (Da Capo Press, New York, 1999)
Lynn, Loretta and Vecsey, George, *Coal Miner's Daughter* (Warner Books, New York, 1977)
Bufwack, Mary A. and Oermann, Robert K., *Finding Her Voice: The Saga of Women in Country Music* (Crown, New York, 1993)
Parton, Dolly, *Dolly—My Life and Other Unfinished Business* (HarperCollins, New York, 1994)

Further Listening
There are literally hundreds of Patsy Cline CDs, but most of them rejig her early 4-Star recordings. MCA Nashville's four-CD set *The Patsy Cline Collection* (1991) is almost definitive, and there are many good single CD collections drawn from her Decca/MCA recordings.

The Maddox Brothers and Rose are best represented by *America's Most Colorful Hillbilly Band* (Arhoolie, 1961, subsequently reissued on CD). Kitty Wells is best represented by *Country Music Hall of Fame* (MCA Nashville, 1991). Wells, incidentally, has also re-recorded her hits, and the remakes usually show up on budget collections. The best sampling of Loretta Lynn's work is on *All Time Greatest Hits* (MCA, 2002). Another MCA CD, *Country Music Hall of Fame* (1991), is a good overview, and MCA's Loretta Lynn boxed set, *Honky Tonk Girl* (1994), includes every hit.

There are over 100 currently available Dolly Parton CDs, but *The Essential Dolly Parton Volumes 1 & 2* (RCA, 1995 and 1997), are probably the best starting point. *Greatest Hits* (RCA, 1982) focuses on her pop recordings. Her later bluegrass CDs for Sugar Hill Records marked a late career resurgence. *Little Sparrow* (2001) is exceptional. Tammy Wynette is best represented by Columbia's *20 Greatest Hits* (1992). For high psychodrama, check out *George and Tammy's Greatest Hits* (Columbia, 1990).

CHAPTER 13
George Jones—born Saratoga, Texas, September 12, 1931.

Johnny Cash—born Kingsland, Arkansas, February 26, 1932.

Further Reading
Jones, George with Carter, Tom, *I Lived to Tell It All* (Villard Books, New York, 1996)
Allen, Bob, *George Jones: The Life and*

Times of a Honky Tonk Legend (Birch Lane Press, New York, 1994)
Cash, Johnny with Carr, Patrick, *Cash—The Autobiography* (new edition, HarperCollins, New York, 2000)

Further Listening
George Jones cries out to be properly anthologized. Columbia/Sony's *The Essential* (1994) recaps the big ones (which aren't necessarily the best ones), and the classic Starday and Mercury sides can be found on a two-CD anthology, *Cup of Loneliness* (Mercury Nashville. 1994). Rhino Records has a single CD Jones anthology, *1955-1967* (1991), overviewing the pre-Columbia era.

From among the 200 or so Johnny Cash albums currently available, Columbia's two-CD *The Essential* (1992) is a good primer of the Sun and Columbia recordings. Columbia/Sony has also reissued a number of Cash's original concept albums, including *Bitter Tears* (1964). Columbia/Sony also tried rethinking Johnny Cash, sorting his songs into three themed collections, *God, Love,* and *Murder*

JOHNNY CASH

(2000). The Sun recordings have been permutated endlessly from budget CDs to a definitive five-CD boxed set, *The Man in Black 1954-1958* (Bear Family, 1988). Cash's first American Records CD, *American Recordings* (1994), is a classic.

CHAPTER 14
Roger Miller—born Fort Worth, Texas, January 2, 1936; died Nashville, October 25, 1992. After a long dry spell in the 1970s, Miller wrote a Broadway musical, *Big River,* based on Mark Twain's *The Adventures of Huckleberry Finn,* which won a Tony award in 1985.

KRIS KRISTOFFERSON

Kris Kristofferson—born Brownsville, Texas, June 22, 1936. In addition to his music career, he has made more than twenty movies, including *Pat Garrett and Billy the Kid, A Star Is Born,* and *Lone Star.*

Glen Campbell—born Delight, Arkansas, April 22, 1936.

Merle Haggard—born Bakersfield, California, April 6, 1937.

Further Reading
Campbell, Glen and Carter, Tom, *Rhinestone Cowboy* (Villard Books, New York, 1994)

Grissim, John, *Country Music, White Man's Blues* (Coronet, New York, 1970)

Haggard , Merle and Russell, Peggy, *Sing Me Back Home* (Crown Publishing, New York, 1981)

Hemphill, Paul, *The Nashville Sound: Bright Lights and Country Music* (Simon & Schuster, New York, 1970)

Further Listening
There are many CDs of Roger Miller's hits, but the best overview of his eccentric life and career is a three-CD box, *King of the Road—The Genius of Roger Miller* (Mercury Nashville, 1995). Kris Kristofferson's best-known work is well represented on *All-Time Greatest Hits* (Varese-Sarabande, 2001), and Glen Campbell's career is neatly synopsized on the two-CD set *The Glen Campbell Collection 1962-1989* (Razor + Tie, 1997). Unsurprisingly, the Reb Rebel recordings and Guy Drake's "Welfare Cadillac" have not been reissued, but Bear Family included Marty Robbins' two far-right recordings on a 1995 boxed set, *Country 1960-1966.* Merle Haggard has re-recorded his hits, so the Capitol reissues are the ones to look for. *Down Every Road* (Capitol Nashville, 1996) is a fine four-CD career overview, and Capitol has also reissued his 1969 album *Okie from Muskogee.* Haggard's later albums, such as *If I Could Only Fly* (Anti Records, 2000), promise a late career surge.

CHAPTER 15
Olivia Newton-John—born Cambridge, England, September 26, 1948. She grew up in Australia and returned to England in 1964. She was in the prefabricated pop group Toomorrow, then toured with Cliff Richard. Her best-known role was in the movie musical *Grease* (1978). An attempt to return to country music in 1998 didn't work.

OLIVIA NEWTON-JOHN

Charlie Rich—born Forrest City, Arkansas, December 14, 1932; died Hammond, Louisiana, July 25, 1995. After his retirement, he recorded just one album, *Pictures and Paintings* (1991), that captured the sprawl of his music.

Conway Twitty—born Harold Lloyd Jenkins in Friars Point, Mississippi, September 1, 1933; died en route home from Branson, Missouri, June 5, 1993.

Gilley's—Houston's biggest tourist attraction in the early 1980s, spawning a syndicated radio show, and line-ups that ran for two blocks. It burned down in 1989, and Gilley later opened his own club in Branson, Missouri.

Further Reading
Cross, Wilbur L. and Kosser, Michael, *Conway Twitty: An Authorized Biography* (Doubleday, New York, 1986)
Davis, Hank, CD notes to *Charlie Rich: Lonely Weekends* (Bear Family Records, 1998)

Further Listening
There appears to be no overview of Olivia Newton-John's country recordings, but her hits are gathered on *Magic: The Very Best Of…* (MCA, 2001). The best way to experience the sprawl of Charlie Rich's career is on Epic Legacy's two-CD *Feel Like Going Home* (1997) or on Hip-O's *Ultimate Collection* (2000). As is so often the case, Conway Twitty re-recorded his hits, so budget CDs should generally be avoided, but there's a good single CD overview of his career, Hip-O's *The Ultimate Collection* (1999), and a four-CD set, *The Conway Twitty Collection* (MCA Nashville, 1995). The *Urban Cowboy* soundtrack (Elektra, 1980) is still available for those who want to re-live the era.

CHAPTER 16
Waylon Jennings—born Wayland Arnold Jennings in Littlefield, Texas, June 13, 1937; died Chandler, Arizona, February 13, 2002.

Billy Joe Shaver—born Corsicana, Texas, August 16, 1939.

Willie Nelson—born Abbott, Texas, April 30, 1933.

Tompall Glaser—born Thomas Paul Glaser in Spalding, Nebraska, September 3, 1933.

David Allan Coe—born Akron, Ohio, September 6, 1939.

Randall "Hank" Williams, Jr.—born Shreveport, Louisiana, September 26, 1949.

Further Reading
Bane, Michael, *The Outlaws: A Revolution in Country Music* (Doubleday, New York, 1978)
Jennings, Waylon with Kaye, Lenny, *Waylon* (Time-Warner International, New York, 1997)
Nelson, Willie with Shrake, Bud, *Willie—An Autobiography* (Cooper Square Publishers, New York, 2000)
Williams, Hank Jr., *Living Proof* (Dell Publishing, New York, 1983)

Further Listening
Wanted! The Outlaws (RCA, 1976) is still available, now with bonus tracks and bonus essays. There are several overviews of Waylon Jennings'

WAYLON JENNINGS

recordings (RCA's 2001 collection, *The Essential,* comprehensively surveys his hits), but the best way to experience his music is through his original mid-1970s' RCA albums, *Dreaming My Dreams* (1975), *This Time* (1974), *The Ramblin' Man* (1974), and *Honky Tonk Heroes* (1973), all reissued with bonus tracks.

From among the 200 Willie Nelson albums currently available, *Red Headed Stranger* (Columbia, 1975) and *Stardust* (Columbia, 1978) should be heard in their entirety. There's a three-CD overview, *Revolutions of Time* (Columbia, 1996) while RCA's *The Essential* (1995) recaps the undervalued RCA years. The two Atlantic albums, *Phases and Stages* (1973) and *Shotgun Willie* (1974), are sporadically available.

Billy Joe Shaver's work is synopsized on Razor + Tie's 1995 set, *Restless Wind 1973-1987,* while Koch has reissued his original Monument album *Old Five and Dimers Like Me* (1973). Tompall Glaser's recordings are only on a Collectors Choice CD, *The Best of Tompall Glaser* (2001), while David Allan Coe's best-known songs are liberally available, often as remakes (the originals are gathered on Columbia/Sony's *17 Greatest Hits,* 1990). There's an almost infinite amount of Hank, Jr. CDs, but Curb Records' inappropriately titled *The Complete* is a three-CD boxed overview (1999).

CHAPTER 17
Emmylou Harris—born Birmingham, Alabama, April 2, 1947. She met Gram Parsons in 1971.

Ricky Skaggs—born Cordell, Kentucky, July 18, 1954. His early partner, Keith Whitley (born Sandy Hook, Kentucky, July 1, 1955), also became a country star, scoring five number one hits in 1988 and 1989, but drank himself to death in Nashville, May 9, 1989.

John Anderson—also known as John David Anderson, born Orlando, Florida, December 13, 1954.

JOHN ANDERSON

George Strait—born Poteet, Texas, May 18, 1952, but raised on a farm near Pearsall, Texas.

Randy Travis—born Randy Traywick, Marshville, North Carolina, May 4, 1959.

Dwight Yoakam—born Pikeville, Kentucky, October 23, 1956.

Steve Earle—born Fort Monroe, Virginia, January 17, 1955, but raised near San Antonio, Texas.

Further Reading
Boxed set notes to George Strait, *Straight Out of the Box* (MCA Records, 1995)

Further Listening
A three-CD Emmylou Harris boxed set, *Portraits* (Warner Archives, 1996) is available, but her music is best represented by the original albums (all on Warner Bros.). *Pieces of the Sky* (1975), *Blue Kentucky Girl* (1979), *Roses in the Snow* (1980), and *Angel Band* (1987) are probably the countriest. Ricky Skaggs is also best served by his original LPs, notably the early duet album with Tony Rice, *Skaggs and Rice* (Sugar Hill, 1980); the first solo album, *Sweet Temptation* (Sugar Hill, 1981); the first hit album *Waitin' for the Sun to Shine* (Columbia, 1981); and his return to bluegrass with *Ancient Tones* (Skaggs Family, 1999). There are two *Greatest Hits* compilations drawn from John Anderson's Warner Bros. recordings (*Volume 1*, 1984 and *Volume 2*, 1990), but *Wild and Blue* (Warner Bros., 1982) is still the one to find.

There has been a George Strait album almost every year since 1976, and from among those *Does Fort Worth Ever Cross Your Mind* (MCA, 1984) stands up well, as does *Beyond the Blue Neon* (MCA, 1989). The 1995 boxed set *Straight out of the Box* (MCA) mixes the big hits with a few rarities, such as an ill-conceived duet with Frank Sinatra. In 2002, Rhino released an encapsulation of Randy Travis's career, *Trail of Memories,* but his first Warners album, *Storms of Life,* remains his finest work. Every Dwight Yoakam album is worth hearing because he has recorded when the albums were ready, not when the company needed the billing. *Guitars, Cadillacs, etc. etc.* (Reprise, 1986) retains its low-fi cowpunk appeal, and

Buenos Noches from a Lonely Room (Reprise, 1988) features the duet with Buck Owens on "Streets of Bakersfield." *Last Chance for a Thousand Years* (Reprise, 1999) recaps his biggest chart hits.

CHAPTER 18
Branson—the story of Branson, Missouri, is recapitulated in *Branson and Beyond* by Kathryn Buckstaff (St Martin's Press, New York, 1973). The Ozark music scene is covered in an article by Dave Hoekstra, "Queen City of the Ozarks," in the *Journal of Country Music,* Volume 22.3 (2002), and in a book by Reta Spears-Stewart, *Remembering the Ozark Jubilee* (Gilead Publishing, Springfield, Missouri, 1993).

CHAPTER 19
Gram Parsons—born Ingram Cecil Connor in Winter Haven, Florida, November 5, 1946; died Joshua Tree, California, September 19, 1973.

Further Reading
Alden, Grant and Blackstock, Peter (eds), *No Depression: An Introduction*

GRAM PARSONS

to *Alternative Country Music, Whatever That Is* (Dowling Press, Nashville, 1998)

Further Listening
Gram Parsons' work with the Flying Burrito Brothers can be found on *Hot Burritos 1969-1972* (A&M, 2000), and his two solo albums, *G.P.* (Reprise, 1973) and *Return of the Grievous Angel* (Reprise, 1974) are now together on one CD. Uncle Tupelo's original *No Depression* LP (Rockville, 1990) goes in and out of print, but there's a compilation, *1989-1993: An Anthology* (Columbia Legacy, 2002). The two acknowledged Lambchop classics are *How I Quit Smoking* (Merge, 1996) and *What Another Man Spills* (Merge, 1998). From among the Paul Burch albums, *Wire to Wire* (Checkered Past, 1998) is probably the best, although *Last of My Kind* (Merge, 2001) is fine. Gillian Welch's three albums, *Revival* (Almo Sounds, 1996), *Hell Among the Yearlings* (Almo, 1998), and her self-

ALAN JACKSON

produced *Time* (Acony, 2001) are all worth owning. Robbie Fulks's music is best represented by *Country Love Songs* (Bloodshot Records, 1996) and *13 Hillbilly Giants* (Boondoggle, 2001).

CHAPTER 20
Garth Brooks—born Troyal Garth Brooks in Luba, Oklahoma, February 7, 1962.

Clint Black—born Long Branch, New Jersey, February 4, 1962, but raised in Houston, Texas. Z. Z. Top's manager, Bill Ham, spotted Black in Houston, and arranged a deal with RCA, Nashville. His first album, *Killin' Time*, proved to be the most successful (certified triple platinum, or 3 million units sold). Subsequent albums veered between country pop and harder country with mixed results, both artistically and commercially. He has ventured into acting on television and in movies.

Vince Gill—born Norman, Oklahoma, April 12, 1957.

Alan Jackson—born Newman, Georgia, October 17, 1958.

Shania Twain—born Eileen Edwards in Windsor, Ontario, Canada, August 28, 1965.

Further Reading
There are "clipping service" biographies of the current major country stars, but there is no recommendable overview of recent years or of recent stars. Clark Parsons' analysis of Shania Twain's breakthrough was published in the *Journal of Country Music,* Volume 18.3 (1996).

CLINT BLACK

Further Listening
Garth Brooks takes his CDs in and out of print, but *No Fences* (Capitol, 1990) and *Ropin' the Wind* (Capitol, 1991) are the ones to own. Brooks' hits album, *The Hits* (Capitol, 1994), was in print for only one year, but sold in excess of 8 million, so can't really be considered a limited edition. Vince Gill recorded two truly great CDs, *When I Call Your Name* (MCA, 1989) and *The Key* (MCA, 1998). He hasn't issued a hits collection since *Souvenirs* (MCA, 1995). Alan Jackson has released almost one album a year since 1990. *A Lot 'bout Livin' and a Little 'bout Love* (Arista, 1992) might still be the best, but they're consistently good. *Under the Influence* (Arista, 1999) is a collection of revivals, cementing Jackson's connection to country music's past. There are essentially two Shania Twain CDs, *The Woman in Me* (Mercury Nashville, 1995) and *Come on Over* (Mercury Nashville, 1999), both commercial juggernauts and both remixed and reconfigured for overseas markets. The accompanying video collections complete the picture.

index

picture credits

Bear Family Archive: 20; 23; 24; 25; 31; 33; 56–7; 63; 75; 95; 96; 102; 103; 130.
Branson Convention and Vistors Bureau: 156.
Colin Escott: 36–7; 46 bottom; 67; 69; 86; 87; 93; 105; 115; 143.
Grand Ole Opry Archive: 4–5; 7; 8; 18; 39; 43; 47; 48; 50–1; 52; 54; 58; 59; 60–1;
64; 65; 66; 68; 70; 74; 76; 77; 78; 78 (inset); 80; 83; 84–5; 91; 92; 98; 99; 100; 101;
106; 109; 110; 112; 113; 116; 119; 124; 127; 128; 132; 139; 140; 147; 148; 151;
157; 164.
Buddy Griffin courtesy of David Dennard: 40.
Lynn McMurry: 15; 44–5; 71; 125 (both).
Mercury Records, Nashville: 170; 173.
Merge Records: 160.
Nashville Banner Collection/Nashville Public Library: 29; 106; 111; 121; 123; 133;
136; 141; 144 (inset).
Michael Ochs Archives: 162.
Peermusic Inc: 21.
Pittsburg State University, Kansas: 27; 38.
Revenant Records: 13.
Allen H. Seffker: 17.
Showtime Music Archive: 16; 30; 46 top; 53; 90; 94; 104; 114; 120; 131; 135; 137;
138; 144; 146; 150; 152 (co-credit Jeffrey Mayer); 154 (co-credit Jeff Katz); 155 (co-
credit Andy Phillips); 164; 166 (co-credit Beverly Parker); 169.
Glenn Sutton: 42; 72–73; 89; 158–9.
University of Louisville/Caufield & Shook Collection: 19; 34.

lyric credits

The Last Letter
Words and Music by Rex Griffin
Copyright 1939 (renewed) Unichappell Music Inc., USA. Warner/Chappell
Music Ltd, London W6 8BS (for US rights only). Reproduced by permission
of International Music Publications Ltd. All Rights Reserved.

Four Walls
Words and Music by Marvin Moore and George Campbell
Copyright 1957 EMI Catalogue Partnership, EMI Unart Catalog Inc. and EMI
United Partnership Ltd, USA. Worldwide print rights controlled by Warner
Bros. Publications Inc/IMP Ltd. Reproduced by permission of International
Music Publications Ltd. All Rights Reserved.

The Fightin' Side of Me
Copyright 1970 Sony/ATV Songs LLC. All rights administered by Sony/ATV
Music Publishing, 8 Music Square West, Nashville, TN 37203. All rights
reserved. Used by permission.

Lost Highway
Copyright 1949 Sony/ATV Acuff Rose Music. All rights administered by
Sony/ATV Music Publishing, 8 Music Square West, Nashville, TN 37203.
All rights reserved. Used by permission.

Please Make up Your Mind
Copyright 1952 Sony/ATV Acuff Rose Music and Hiriam Music. All rights on
behalf of Sony/ATV Acuff Rose Music administered by Sony/ATV Music
Publishing, 8 Music Square West, Nashville, TN 37203. All rights reserved.
Used by permission.

Wildwood Flower (A. P. Carter)
Peermusic

This Cold War with You (Floyd Tillman)
Peermusic

Every effort has been made to contact all copyright holders. The publishers
would be pleased to hear if any oversights or omissions have occurred.